The Fight
for Democracy

The Fight for Democracy

The Libertas Voice in Europe

A series of interviews
with Declan Ganley

by Bruce Arnold

Kilynton
HouseBooks

First published 2009 by Killynon House Books Ltd.

ISBN: 978-1-905706-18-1

Printed and bound in the EU by CPI

KILLYNON HOUSE BOOKS
Killynon, Turin, Mullingar, Co. Westmeath, Ireland
Email: khbooks@iol.ie

About the author

Bruce Arnold is a political columnist with the *Irish Independent*. Arnold has written more than 15 books, including biographies of Charles Haughey, Jack Lynch and Margaret Thatcher

CONTENTS

FOREWORD

Declan Ganley was the most successful Irish political campaigner of 2008.

While the country watched other political leaders fumbling their way into the Lisbon Treaty referendum – which was the biggest issue of the first half of the year – Ganley focused his Libertas movement in a clear and exclusive way on what was wrong with the European Union and mounted a campaign that was unwavering in its presentation. He undoubtedly led the disparate No vote parties and groups but did so in a detached way, making no alliances and emerging as the real heart of doubt and disillusionment, while at the same time saying there was a better way.

He won. The others lost. The Government made a mess of the campaign. Fianna Fail were lukewarm and over-confident. Fine Gael were uncertain and divided. The Labour Party also had mixed views. The Green Party – committed to being 'in government' for what it called 'the long haul' – went against their earlier doubts but presented no convincing campaign. Sinn Fein's opposition was in keeping with its traditional nationalism but it was limited because of the party's association with the Northern Ireland troubles.

The victory for the No vote, though it was the principal achievement in Declan Ganley's political success last year, was not a solo achievement. There was deep-seated public suspicion about the European Union and what it now stands for that had little to do with campaigning organizations. There were widespread doubts about the levels of democracy espoused by Brussels. It seemed that the Commission, the Council of Ministers and the bureaucracy governing us from Brussels, Strasbourg and Luxembourg, had a distinctly cool view about the nature and interpretation of democratic answerability and transparency. They insisted on it for Member States. It was a primary requirement in the accession process for new members. But many of the elements in what was demanded from past and future EU members did not apply to the central government of the EU itself.

This was indeed part of Declan Ganley's argument, but it was an argument much more widely held among voters and proved conclusive in the result. To an astonishing degree it was not addressed by arguments from the Yes vote side. Jobs, grants, preferential treatment, favourable tax provisions, the veto, Ireland 'being at the heart of Europe', Ireland owing a Yes vote in response to the huge help given to the country from our accession in 1973: all these were put forward. But no one seemed to think of the democratic issue. The campaign touched on the idea that 'more democracy' had been 'granted' under the Lisbon Treaty, as if democracy was like European grant-aid – something that had to be rationed.

Declan Ganley consistently argued that this was not enough. The democratic deficit was much deeper than that and required, in the first instance, the rejection of a Treaty that would stifle all future efforts to change Europe into a true democracy. How this would be done was open to question. But that it needed to be done was increasingly realized as the campaign progressed.

The second half of 2008 descended into financial crisis and the Lisbon Treaty was rendered more defective and irrelevant as Europe itself floundered. But before this happened the Cowen-led government made the extraordinary mistake of indicating – almost before all the votes had been counted in the referendum poll – that there would be an attempt to reverse the decision. Taoiseach Brian Cowen seems to have told Gordon Brown to go ahead with British ratification of the Lisbon Treaty because Ireland would eventually ratify following a re-run referendum and this indication was relayed to Europe generally, supported with some determination by the Minister for Foreign Affairs, Micheál Martin.

What might have passed over, with the decline in activity of Libertas and other proponents of the No vote, went in an entirely different direction. The Government could have achieved their objectives much more subtly by ensuring that the motivation for trying again came from Europe and was put to a reluctant Irish Government trying their best to stand behind a democratic decision of the State. Instead, Dublin led the charge. This probably astonished Europe. It certainly got a warm response from the French, who held the EU presidency, and Nicolas Sarkozy visited Dublin to reinforce Europe's support for a reconsideration of the referendum decision.

This brought Declan Ganley back in an even stronger position, confirming him in his earlier declared intention of Libertas seeking European Parliament seats and continuing to fight for a better and more democratic EU that way.

The Government made further mistakes, notably in pretending that they had obtained large and valuable concessions from Brussels at the December Summit, when in fact they had obtained trivial political promises that would leave the Lisbon Treaty unchanged, which they dressed up as major achievements. The question of democracy in Brussels was still ignored, not just by Ireland's politicians but by most of the media as well.

It seemed that Declan Ganley still had a voice in Europe and was still determined to exercise it in the forthcoming European election. It was against this background that I decided that it was both a matter of public interest and a journalistic duty to investigate the man, his party and his political intentions. Declan Ganley's Voice in Europe needed to be tested and examined.

A huge amount of negative information, much of it in the form of smears, innuendoes and outright lies, has followed his convincing success last June. A good deal of it has come from officials in Europe, politicians in the European Parliament and from several of the Irish political parties. There has also been a media campaign against him.

From my point of view it seemed that the best way to do this was by interrogation in the form of interviews, which began in January 2009. They mainly cover the European Union and its defects but they also deal with wider issues on which Declan Ganley has been misrepresented or criticised.

What follows is the result.

Bruce Arnold, March 2009

1

DEMOCRACY AND THE EU COMMISSION

Your political career has been largely built around the issue of democracy. How does it work in Europe? Is there really a democratic deficit? Is it serious? Can it be put right? How should this be done?

The problem with the current approach in the European Union is that there is no will in favour of democracy. There is some democracy, of course. We have it in the European Parliament. We have it, to a lesser extent, in the Council of Ministers. But the attitude of the European Union, as an entity, is to dish out democracy in packages, as though it were a grant. Democracy, in anything truly recognisable as such, is approaching an end in Brussels. The Lisbon Treaty would end it. And I simply don't know how we would get democracy restored once power has been gifted to undemocratic institutions which have a proven track record for making the transition from being simply undemocratic to becoming actively anti-democratic as evidenced by the way they ignored and sought to overturn the democratic decisions of the peoples of France, the Netherlands and Ireland in relation to the EU Constitution/Lisbon Treaty.

It is this anti-democratic approach I seek to challenge. The EU requires all her Member-States to be democratic. It does not offer a choice of different forms of democracy. It requires the governments of Member States to be elected by universal suffrage and to form the governments in each state on the basis of majority rule.

No such system applies to the Union itself. That is the heart of the democratic deficit. If the European Union sought EU membership the EU would have to turn itself down. Its democratic standards are utterly defective and getting worse. We have to fix this now, not later, now. It's gone too far.

Can we begin with your own definitions? I will then come to your criticisms of what has gone wrong. Where did you get your own understanding of democracy?

In school and later in life through regular day-to-day experience, I learned the essentials of democracy. All public power derives from the people. For example, in Ireland it is confirmed in Article 6 of the Irish Constitution: 'All powers of government, legislative, executive and judicial, derive, under God, from the people, whose right it is to designate the rulers of the State and, in final appeal, to decide all questions of national policy, according to the requirements of the common good.'

This very strong sentence from the Irish Constitution represents the core of the democracy I was brought up to cherish. All Irish public institutions exist to serve the people. That is the way things operate in Ireland and if it were not so it would be a legitimate task of the people to make it so. The word 'Minister' means servant. Ministers should and shall serve the people. And in the end, we – the voters –decide all public affairs.

Can this lack of democracy be put right?

No one has the right to govern us without our consent. No longer are emperors, kings, noblemen or dictators born to govern us, without reference to the ballot box. We, the citizens, are all fundamentally equal and all power derives from the people. Every one of us has one vote each when we go to the ballot box and delegate legislative power to the elected members of our parliament. If we are not satisfied with our representatives we can vote them out and replace them at the next election. Because our politicians know they have to be re-elected they have to listen to us also between elections. We are supposed to hold the ultimate sanction, otherwise it is not democracy.

In Ireland, we can follow the debates on all laws in the Dáil. Our media do that for us. Our business organisations and trade unions have staff to track law-making. We can send representatives to influence law-making before laws are made. We can debate and scrutinise proposals in public. We can even organize demonstrations and use our freedom of expression to influence the legislative power of our country. All power originates from and belongs to us, the citizens.

This simple and great idea of democracy was born in Athens in ancient Greece, now more than 2,500 years ago. We may be dissatisfied with failures in our own society, but it is our own fault and responsibility if we do not try to change it. We can bring about positive change, indeed, we must. Putting this right starts with understanding how badly things have gone wrong.

Do you think mending our national democracy is possible?

Yes. We *can* and *must* change. Obama won the presidency of the most powerful country on earth, and did it against the odds. He did it on the claim that he could bring 'Change to America'. Of course it remains to be seen what such change will produce. Voters and historians will give their eventual verdict. For my part I wish him every success.

In my day-to-day life and with some reading, I also

learned about the division of power between legislative, executive and judicial powers. This idea was coined by the French philosopher, Montesquieu, who wrote a book entitled *On the Spirit of the Laws*.

How did he define the workings of government?

His proposition was that, for a democracy to flourish, the three branches or powers of government should be separated to avoid abuse and to prevent any one dimension being dominant.

The legislative body, the Parliament, should decide laws – under the control of voters, who would elect its members. The executive body, the Government, should implement the law – under control of Parliament. Independent judges should then adjudicate the various and conflicting interpretations of law and monitor the executive Government and the Parliament to make sure that all institutions respect the fundamental rights of citizens according to our constitution.

This division of power into these three branches is tried and tested common sense. It provides an essential safeguard for us, the citizens. In the end, no power can exist against the will of the majority of our citizens. This is the core of democracy, and this is what unites all Member States in the family of the European Union.

But you say it does not work for Europe, for the EU itself?

No country can enter the European Union without subscribing to these basic principles of democracy. The paradox is that these democratic principles are not followed by the Union itself in its own structures and institutions.

As I said, if the EU were to ask for membership in the Union we, the people, in our exercise of democracy, would simply have to say: 'Sorry, EU, you do not come close to meeting the requirements that qualify you as a democracy.'

So, let's start with the Commission. What do we have to do to put right the European Commission?

A commission is usually an advisory body. A political commission would prepare drafts of legislation and advise on their implementation. Specialists might come together and prepare important laws. The various political parties might be represented in a law-preparing commission. By the end of the preparatory process the elected government would then draft a proposal for a law and send it for deliberation in the parliament. Finally, the parliament would decide the content in different readings.

And the EU Commission does more than this?

The Commission in Brussels is much more than a preparatory and advisory body. I was stunned when I discovered it can even decide many laws on its own – so-called delegated legislation. And all of this by the unelected. It's a lobbyists' dream! They are lobbying lawmakers that never have to face an electorate. That's a dish for corruption if ever there was one. It's no wonder the EU did not have its accounts signed off by its own auditors for 13 years.

Where does the Commission structure come from?

The Brussels Commission is composed of one member from each of the 27 Member States. The Irish member of the Commission is currently appointed by the Irish Government. Charlie McCreevy is Ireland's present Commissioner. He was formerly Minister for Finance. As our European Commissioner he has responsibility for the

Internal Market. It is an important portfolio, and administered by an Irishman, though it should be pointed out his first loyalty is to the EU.

He and most of his colleagues originated in national elections many years ago, but they are no longer answerable to an electorate. On occasion, they may even have been appointed to the Commission because the Government wanted to be rid of a person for various reasons. The former British Commissioner Peter Mandelson was rejected as Minister twice in the UK and then sent to Brussels by Tony Blair. We have had similar situations in the past. There was even speculation that McCreevy, a capable Minister for Finance, was sidelined when he was moved to Brussels.

How do you argue that the Brussels Commission is not democratic?

In a democracy we vote for lawmakers in elections, but we never vote for EU Commissioners. And we cannot get rid of them as we can get rid of a TD/MP by voting him or her out of office.

Let's look at what happens under the Lisbon Treaty. The Nice Treaty gave the Irish Government the right to appoint the Irish Commissioner. This right is removed under the Lisbon Treaty. That means *less* 'democracy'. Under Lisbon our Government can only put forward 'suggestions' for who our Commissioner should be. Someone else has the right, and the power, to decide. Today, under the Treaty of Nice, the Irish Government can put forward proposals and can actually decide who its national Commissioner is.

Under the Lisbon Treaty it would be up to the newly appointed (not elected) Commission President to choose the Irish man or woman who will be a member of the next

European Commission. How is that democratic?

But surely, as you have said, the EU Commissioners are loyal to the EU, not to Ireland?

That is not the public perception, though it may be the legal position. If we abide by the legal position, then why do we want to have our own Commissioner? The answer is obvious: we do not want to follow the legal position. We think having our own Commissioner bestows some sort of benefit. Yet no one knows quite what it is. This is the first of many anomalies in the EU system that seem deliberately to have been left ambiguous.

How does the Brussels Commission work?

Every new Commission is approved by a special qualified majority of 20 of the 27 Prime Ministers. They will take the decision on who its members are behind closed doors at a summit of the European Council. The new Commission has also to be supported as a whole by an absolute majority of members in the European Parliament.

But doesn't that sound like a democratic process?

It looks democratic when you read in the Lisbon Constitution that the European Parliament 'elects' the Commission. But it only elects them as a full group after the individual members of the group have first been chosen by the EU Prime Ministers in the European Council. You also have to know what happens if the Parliament does not approve the proposed full Commission. The answer is: nothing. The elected members of the European Parliament cannot install another Commission President or an alternative EU government. They have a quaint source of reserve power: they can reject the full Commission but they cannot elect a new Commission.

This is reminiscent of the so-called 'people's democracies' of Eastern Europe. They could elect those who were put forward by the Communist Party and their allies. The voters in these countries had no free choice to elect whoever they thought would serve them best.

Is this not a form of totalitarianism?

People don't like that term. It offers a valid parallel, but its associations are unacceptable. Nevertheless, it is useful to think along the lines indicated by this form of government in which no genuine opposition operates and if one attempts to start such opposition, a concerted attempt is mounted to crush it. In spite of not being elected, the EU Commission is charged with the sole right of proposing all important laws in Europe and it decides many laws on its own in the form of delegated legislation. It is now the case that the vast majority of new laws, in all 27 Member States of the EU, come from Brussels and are initated by people who never face election or democratic accountability.

In democracies we vote for those who can propose and decide the laws. In the EU today no one we directly vote for is able to propose any law. There are only 27 European citizens, the EU Commission members, with the right to propose a new law or amend an existing law. This is called the Commission's 'monopoly of initiative'. This is not just an unimportant theory. Not even the Taoiseach and his colleagues in the European Council and their ministerial colleagues in other Councils have any right to propose a European law or propose an amendment to an existing law.

Can you spell out the way EU laws are made?

The Prime Ministers or other Ministers can only ask the Commission to put forward an amendment or a new proposal. But it is the non-elected Commissioners who decide if they want to follow ministerial wishes or not. It is utterly ridiculous and dangerous that you have to be non-elected to initiate a law in Brussels, where now the majority of our new laws are made. There is no other way. Democratic law-making is a thing of the past. Clause-by-clause debate on a proposed law will never take place.

Why has this imperfect way of EU law-making not come out, either in the referendum last June, or when the Irish Government discussed things afterwards with the EU Prime Ministers?

The answer is simple. To any right-minded democrat, this way of making law is a fundamental and serious reason for rejecting the Lisbon Treaty. But for those who seek power under the Lisbon Treaty – including some in the present Government – there is no answer. So they were all silent on the issue. No supporter of the Lisbon Treaty wants to admit to this devastating fact, indeed most are entirely unaware of it. So all the Treaty's supporters, with their different reasons for supporting it, were silent on this central problem. They either did not know (in the majority of cases) or they did not want people to know. No Lisbon Treaty supporter could even admit to being aware of this essential defect in EU law-making, because being aware of it meant you had scant regard for democracy.

Why was there no debate on the issue of EU law-making?

The EU does not want its law-making processes debated. It took me weeks, and some metaphorical bruisings, to grasp this absurd reality. You end up having to pinch yourself because it's almost unbelievable that such a bald-faced attempt can be made to usurp fundamental democratic accountability. I don't even know that it is deliberate. I can only think that, seeing how some are so virulently trying to defend it, it might be. It seems to me utterly unacceptable and indefensible in the Europe of the 21st Century.

Are there parallels for this absence of democracy?

Not in the democratic world there aren't. I can find no other place where so much power is given to non-elected persons. In democracies executive power is normally controlled by the parliament. Laws are initiated and decided by the elected members of those parliaments.

In the EU the legislative power is fundamentally linked to the non-elected 'bureaucrats' in Brussels. The Commissioners are members of a college meeting every Tuesday under the leadership of José Manuel Barroso – a former Maoist Communist and a former Prime Minister of Portugal – who has governed the present Commission since 2004.

And that is how they govern? And how do they vote?

Formally the Commission makes its decisions by simple majority vote among the Commissioners. I have been told that there has not been one single vote since 2004, the current Commission period. But in fact only a tiny fraction of Commission decisions are decided by the Commissioners themselves.

In practice, most Commission decisions are made in writing between members of their 'cabinets' or by director-generals or their civil servants in the name of the Commission. Often the Commissioners are not able to govern their own departments. Civil servants behind the scenes, whom we do not know and cannot keep accountable, in reality make most decisions in the name of the institution called the European Commission. Non-elected and non-accountable bureaucrats control the monopoly of initiative in European lawmaking. And that is nuttier than a 'Snickers' bar.

What can you do to change this?

Votes always count. They are the force that shape power. All things can be changed if we have the courage to speak up and defend truth and freedom.

If the EU were invented today no one would give this much power to non-elected people. This abuse of democracy has to be stopped and then reversed. This can only be done if political power is given back to the people. But it will be difficult. The Commission has gained so much power and has passed a tilt point, going from undemocratic to being actively anti-democratic as evidenced by the way they have taken a contemptuous short-cut through the referendum results in France, the Netherlands and Ireland. It would require a unanimous decision amongst all the Member States to modify the monopoly of initiative. This leads one to the conclusion that it would be more realistic to have the Commission democratically elected instead.

How should democratic elections of EU Commissioners be approached?

There are two possible paths. The first is to have a directly elected Commission. The second is for the European Parliament to elect the Commission just like the Dáil elects the Irish Government.

In Europe this latter method is proposed by many so-called 'federalists'. In this way we could establish a European parliamentary democracy just as we have an Irish parliamentary democracy. Those that don't like that idea then need to realize that one way or another the issue has to be faced. You either return power and accountability to the National Parliaments – I would call that the Eurocritical or Eurosceptical approach – or you agree that it makes sense to make some important decisions at the EU level. I would call that the pro-European approach though it could be called a democratic federalist one.

Would it then be a real European Parliamentary democracy? Would it also work to the satisfaction of the voters in 27 very different Member States?

It is a mammoth task. I readily admit that. How many Irishmen would go and vote for Peter Mandelson or José Manuel Barroso? I cannot see any European people, as yet, prepared for true European elections and a true European parliamentary democracy. But of course that could change. It could even be a quick change, depending on events.

The first opportunity for bringing this about might be to propose that the President of the Commission, or the Council of Ministers, be directly elected. I would make this part of a short Constitution or a basic EU Treaty instead of the vast Lisbon Treaty. Of course voters would have the right to reject this idea at the ballot box, but the point is this: if Europe is to have a president on the lines proposed by Lisbon, that person must be accountable to voters or the position should not exist. That was what gave Obama his enormous power. I see that as a remarkable case of 'people-power' in America, but I see that it is not available to the 500-million population of the EU.

Is there an alternative way of democratising the Commission?

What I propose is this – and it is both possible and easy to realise: every country should elect its own

Commissioner in a direct election together with the elections to the European Parliament every five years. It would be a popular choice, fixed in time, as the European elections are fixed. This would engage voters. It would make for a higher turnout and it would also increase public participation in the European elections.

We do not even need to wait for an EU decision to allow such a development. We could simply organise the election of the new Irish Commissioner on our own next time around and thereby inspire other Member States by example to do the same. A Commissioner with an electoral mandate would be very hard for Brussels to reject. If we elected the Irish Commissioner everyone else would eventually have to do the same. European public opinion would be mobilised on the matter.

How would this solve the problem of a democratic mandate?

The proposal would give us a directly elected representative in the powerful body of the European Commission. We would have to change the Treaty rules for deciding on Commissioners. We would have to make them answerable to their own electorates. This would be a fundamental change in the Treaties, but it would also be the proper extension of democratic choice.

This raises the issue of the present situation, where we have 'our' Irish Commissioner, but he isn't technically ours at all. Instead, we would empower our Commissioner by providing him or her with a democratic mandate. Ireland's Commissioner would be answerable, amongst others, for the present monopoly situation of proposing EU laws along with elected Commissioners from the other Member States. Political parties, various movements and alliances, could then put forward their preferred candidates and tour the country and lay out their stall to the voters.

How would the elected EU Commissioners keep in touch with voters?

That would be the Irish Commissioner's responsibility. In addition, he or she could visit the Dáil regularly and answer questions. He or she would report to our elected members of the Dáil as well as to the media.

A reform like this would mean that, for the first time, the Irish Commissioner would actually represent Irish voters. The Irish people would have a direct line into the Commission and into the process of deliberating on European law proposals in the Commission College.

Are there other advantages to this proposal?

A Commissioner with an electoral mandate is going to be harder for the bureaucrats to ignore. The risk of corruption would be lessened, since the Commission would have to consider the inevitable electoral scrutiny and media focus that would follow any newly elected Commission. It would utterly transform the monopoly of initiative principle, making the new system infinitely preferable to what we have now.

At present Charlie McCreevy has the European responsibility for the Internal Market. Irish voters do not have any right to influence him. Nor does anyone else except, perhaps, various lobbyists. What he does is to decide on behalf of all European citizens. Those citizens have no right to intervene.

Would the Commissioner's independence disappear?

It disappeared long ago. It is one of the drawbacks resulting from lack of transparency in the EU that we are not told of the 'national mandate' adopted when it suits countries, in collaboration with their own Commissioners, to disregard their supposed loyalty to Europe and to take instructions from their home-country governments.

It is a known fact that this already happens.

My proposal would simply bring the existing, hidden links between Commissioners and national Governments to public knowledge and make them legitimate. Lobbyists in Brussels would hate it, but that's just tough. It means the lobbyists will have to work harder and they won't get as many bad initiatives through so transparent a system as they do today.

What was behind the Treaty provision for the independence of the Commission?

It was to allow the Brussels Bureaucracy to have absolute control over each of the Commissioners' portfolios, ruling out independence of thought by separating each Commissioner from his or her country of origin. It was an anti-democratic sleight-of-hand. It made Irish voters feel even more distant from the Commission, lessening voters' ability to intervene in the place where all proposals for EU laws originate.

Under Libertas's proposed reform the Lisbon Treaty's concept of independence applying to the Irish Commissioner's administration of his or her European portfolio would be replaced by a system of direct democratic action in the Commission by a representative of Ireland.

This is the way in which the maintenance of a Commissioner for every Member State would make democratic sense. The achievement of this would be a consequence of one of the Libertas campaign slogans: 'Keep Our Commissioner.' It would be a more genuine reform than what gave rise to the trumpeting and self-congratulation of Micheál Martin and Brian Cowen at the December 2008 EU Summit. Let's not kid ourselves. The only reason Brussels backed down on their efforts to deny each Member State a voice at the Commission table was because of the Libertas campaign.

How would reforming the Commission work in practice?

The Libertas proposal on this issue would mean that the administration of the European portfolios by the various Commissioners would have three levels of democratic answerability: the first would be to the Commissioner's own electorate; the second would be to the European Parliament; and the third would be to the Council of Ministers.

How would this change the Commission?

In respect of accountability to Irish voters, they would have influence on proposals for European laws. Obviously they cannot have a monopoly in deciding what their Commissioner would do with the whole internal market. This is Charlie McCreevy's own current responsibility under the Treaties, where he must implement existing European laws. But it would influence law-making in the same way. The ballot box influences anyone accountable to it. This is too precious a democratic right to let it be done without supervision. At present this is carried out privately, secretly and then implemented without what is called 'fuss'. 'Fuss' is often what good democracy is about. While Brussels likes to talk about efficiency in decision-making democracy is not supposed to be 'efficient' as, by design, it requires challenge, debate and opposition. Dictators are 'efficient' in their decision-making because there is no opposition.

Who would preside over the European Commission under Libertas's proposed reform?

We have three models available. We can continue as today when the 27 Prime Ministers meet in the European Council and appoint the Commission President in a vote by qualified majority, which would disadvantage smaller countries even more under Lisbon. We could also ask the European political parties to put forward their candidates for the President of the Commission in the European elections. The President would then be chosen by an alliance representing the majority of seats from the European elections in all Member States. I would like to see something like this as it would add an important and exciting dynamic to Europe and I suspect would fire up the electorate to truly feel that the European Union belongs to them. Another alternative could allow for the 27 elected members of the Commission to elect their own Chairman to govern the college. That would make for a less prestigious President, a *primus inter pares*, the choice of his or her colleagues.

What is your preference for deciding the Commission?

My personal preference would be to see direct elections in Member States of their national Commissioner. That would put democracy at the centre, changing the structure of the EU. It would mean a workable relationship between the European Parliament and the Commission. The Commission President could then be elected by the European Parliament, or the Commission President's and Council President's roles could be merged – but there may be reasons why this might not work. If voters opted for an elected President of the Council, in this case such a democratically elected President should be limited to only one term of office, for no longer than six years. Six years is long enough to get stuff done without being long enough to do long-term, irreversible damage. The strict, one-term limit would mean long-term decisions could be made without the politicking of running for re-election a year or two into office.

2

DEMOCRACY, THE EU COUNCIL OF MINISTERS AND THE EUROPEAN PARLIAMENT

You have made a strong case that the Commission is not democratic while at the same time wielding powers that we reserve for our elected representatives. Surely it is different with the Council of Ministers?

Not really. The Council of Ministers is not very democratic. In many ways it operates like a rubber stamp. In our everyday language – and in its use in local government and in large organizations – a council is an advisory body. In the EU the Council of Ministers has the same role as the Irish Parliament but performs it differently. The Council of Ministers in Brussels decides the laws on the basis of a proposal from the European Commission. This is entirely wrong. Neither body is equipped for the drafting of laws. This means that in practice EU law-making is mainly the work of unknown, remote officials, with even less of a mandate than Commissioners now have.

Most people think that European laws are made by the European Parliament. But this is at minimum a fundamental misunderstanding. It is possibly more than that. There is a kind of subterfuge in the claim made by knowledgeable and experienced 'Europhiles' that, somehow, the Lisbon Treaty improves democracy in the EU because it makes minor changes in the operation of the European Parliament. But the democratic deficit is so great that these are just like a rearrangement of deck-chairs on the Titanic.

What do you mean by that?

I mean that the real legislative power in the European Union is shared between the non-elected Commission and the Ministers and their civil servants in the Council of Ministers. The European Parliament is outside that power-loop and our elected MEPs are really just puppies barking at the moon, yelping about the good they do when, in fact, they are largely impotent but are kept well enough fed to stay contentedly on the leash.

So why is Libertas standing candidates in constituencies and seeking to join the 'puppies'?

Because I believe that, with the will of the people, it can all be changed and the Parliament, particularly when newly-elected with a significant group of Libertas MEPs, has behind it the impetus of a quite different vote. This will not be a pro-Lisbon Constitution vote or a vote for more power for non-elected people in Brussels. At present our elected MEPs are not allowed to follow the negotiations on new laws that are part of the so-called 'service structure' on legislation for the Council of Ministers and the Commission. The members of the European Parliament have no access to this process of negotiation, nor to the negotiating room. It is an absurd situation and turns democracy on its head. We need to turn these MEPs into big dogs that have bite and that respond to the commands of the electorate.

Is it like the Irish Government deciding on the future of the Irish economy in the present crisis, but doing so with the Social Partners instead of with the Dáil?

You could say that. There are close parallels with the ways in which democracy has been deliberately undermined, and particularly so during the long period in which

Fianna Fail have been in power. We don't really have opposition any more, just a political cartel. They rely all too much on making deals behind closed doors. But there has been a general drift away from parliamentary democracy and towards an old-fashioned and, to me, deplorable form of 'corporatism', the cartel, which some of the dimmer bulbs tend to like, but which in the long run ends up spoiling everything: business life, the economy, law-making, regulations, all the things where the EU should be helping the people.

From first-hand experience I can tell you that it's ironic that the most closed-shop, insular, backward, antiquated and self-preserving, protectionist 'industry' in Europe is politics. The way these people protect themselves from competitition, business would rightly be prosecuted, fined and jailed for it. You see the Commission giving a hard time to firms like Ryanair and Microsoft and yet, as one of many examples, in Malta the two main political parties actually own the two main TV and Radio stations, and no one says a word. The examples go on and on. You should try to set up a political party across many of the Member States of the European Union – and then you'll see the barriers to competition that these politicians have erected to protect themselves. It is outrageous.

Each Member State is represented by its own Minister in the Council of Ministers. Those Ministers come from the governments of the Member States and they are responsible to the National Parliaments. Is that not democratic enough?

In theory, yes. The Irish Ministers meeting in the Council represent the Irish Government, which is responsible to the Dáil back in Dublin. And in theory, at the next polling day we can get rid of a Minister who did not represent us well in the EU Council. But there is no way of checking him or her in any detail, either before or after. Because the deliberations at EU level are unreported and unrecorded, we have to rely on the Minister's own interpretation of what he or she achieved, and we know what an unreliable yardstick that would be. Ministers coming back from Council meetings make no formal report that can be checked against the facts because we do not know the facts. So the good interpretation is all pure theory and the bad interpretation – which is the reality – is altogether different. We have no way of knowing how Irish Ministers represent Ireland in the Council. Its deliberations are secret.

But what about the debate on protocols and amendments to persuade the Irish people to change their Lisbon Treaty vote? Was that not very open, the results immediately relayed in detail to the public?

Of course it was a virtuoso performance, in this case, giving us nothing we don't already have. And we all know why. When it suits the Council of Ministers or the Commission they are more than ready to tell all. When it does not suit them, the matter is kept under wraps. There are a number of recent examples. The most recent – and of exceptional interest to Ireland – was the openness with which the Council of Ministers spelt out the 'deals' that would be done to try to change minds in Ireland in a second Lisbon referendum. It was a dishonest attempt at persuasion. For Ireland it was meant to represent an answer to a European problem, not an Irish one. We had decided on Lisbon but Brussels did not accept the decision and is seeking to change it. I won't predict here what could happen but I do know that everything about this attempted referendum re-run is morally and democratically wrong and transactionally dishonest.

Is this absence of democracy confirmed in the Lisbon Treaty?

The general situation is overwhelmingly against transparency and openness. All that we have learned from history about the working of democracy is set aside. And you have to remember, as I said earlier, it's a condition of membership of the Union for a Member State to be a democracy.

In the Council of Ministers no real negotiations take place, except very rarely. The draft EU laws are all prepared, completed and offered for confirmation or final, marginal discussion by something like 300 working groups under the Council. The structure and membership of these groups is not secret. You can find the list on the website of the Council. However, their discussions and working documents are secret.

No truly democratic Parliament in the world would accept such a system. Those working groups are deliberately stacked with civil servants from different Ministries of the Member States. I have met them on flights to Brussels. They constitute a faceless multitude of bureaucrats, writing, editing, discussing and finalising the laws that control ever more of what we do.

Are you suggesting that these working groups, which you describe as 'stacked with civil servants', wield the real power?

It is quite obvious that it is these secretive working groups that really decide the majority of European laws. Yet, like so much else, it's tough to prove it because it is kept under wraps, secretive to the point of being Machiavellian. When their deliberations come to the

Council of Ministers for formal adoption, they come as so-called 'A-Points', which are not discussed at all, or 'B Points', which are down for formal discussion. And most of the latter are rarely voted on, but adopted by consensus as people look around the table and see how the votes would stack up if someone pushed things to a vote. Small countries are very slow to do the latter.

And all of this is contained in the Lisbon Treaty? Are we voting for a secret 'Government of Europe'?

We already have that. We are confirming it, and making the act of submission part of our Constitution. It has always been developed along these lines, which is why I now so strongly object to it, as would any right-thinking European. The situation is this: all decisions in the Council are prepared in advance. This is done, as you say, in secret. The process is completely unknown to the public. The civil servants even call themselves 'ministers' and they form a sort of government, and it's a bloody powerful one. It decides many more laws than the Dáil. It has a name, 'Coreper', which stands for the Committee of Permanent Representatives, and is composed of an ambassador from each country.

You make it sound like a secret society. Is that fair?

I am only telling you the fact of what is. It obviously isn't a secret society but its structures and approach are odd. It's the result of the compound effect of one bad decision piled on top of another that has produced this unacceptable way of doing things. The four different Coreper groups on average meet once a day from Monday to Thursday. They decide, within their working groups, the vast majority of European laws. As I have said, only a minority of the laws are ever even discussed in the

Council itself. Even fewer lead to real negotiations between Ministers at the Council level. Even here there are very few real negotiations among Ministers on new European laws; many barely get reviewed at all, sometimes getting literally seconds of consideration and no debate whatsoever.

What is Libertas's alternative? How should it happen?
First of all, it should be open to press coverage and to surveillance by MEPs. Secondly, the deliberations should all be recorded. The Union decides around 3000 new laws per year. Only some 50 actually come to a formal vote in a European Council meeting. This allows some public knowledge of the small number of countries voting against any of these very few laws.

Otherwise, the laws are decided in ways that very few Ministers are able to explain. There are also many different rules for EU decision-making in different circumstances. No one can remember all the rules. This is clearly evident from reading the Treaties.

When there is a Council of Ministers vote, what happens?
The most important procedure is based on the principle of 'qualified majority voting'. In this, every Member State gets a number of votes. The Irish Minister – this means, in reality in most cases, an Irish civil servant – has seven votes at his disposal. His Belgian equivalent has 10 votes, the British and the Germans have 29 votes each. There are 345 votes in total and a European law is passed when it gets 255 votes.

And is that how Europe runs us all? Is that the source of the multitude of rules and regulations which govern so

many things in trade, commerce, the environment, factory and shop management, so many things we do?

Don't ask, I cannot tell you why. This is just how it is. It's just as important to know this EU voting rule as the simple majority rule everyone knows about from the Dáil. To block an EU law – meaning one of the few laws that actually comes to a vote – requires 91 votes. This is worked out by subtracting 255 from 345 and adding one. The civil servants who run this system call this unknown magic number the 'blocking minority'.

So Ireland has no veto on EU laws?

The Irish Minister – which normally means the civil servant who is, theoretically, under Government or Departmental instruction – is unable to block a law on his own. The so-called 'veto right' for each Member State on so-called 'vital issues' disappeared in 1987. There are now only vetoes when a decision requires 'unanimity' among the Member States and that is expressly stated in the Treaties and, of course, these areas are hugely reduced under the Lisbon Treaty.

Can you give an example?

I can say this: I was more than a little surprised when the IFA Chairman said he had 'secured the veto' in relation to the Lisbon Treaty debate in Ireland where no such veto existed. He'd been sold a pig in a poke, but he wanted to believe it and farmers ended up being misled by the Government and at that stage even by the IFA Chairman. We even got evidence from Brussels backing our position and the Government still denied it.

How do European laws get blocked?

It is all done by wheeler-dealing. Nowadays, a Minister

can only hinder a decision by qualified majority if he can convince countries with a total of 91 votes. And our Government couldn't convince them it was raining on a wet day. Now get this: a law from the Dáil can be outlawed by majority vote in the EU Council. How many punters do you think are aware of that? Because if they were, there would have been very few votes in favour of the Lisbon Treaty.

Would the position get worse under the Lisbon Treaty?

The Lisbon Treaty would significantly increase those policy areas for decision by qualified majority vote at EU level. It would dramatically reduce the areas requiring unanimity. That way it would become much easier to have decisions taken against the wishes of the Dáil. Mind you, the Dáil is all the time being made more irrelevant, with decisions being made outside it. But that's not my battle. The European Union situation is much more serious and perilously close to a point of no return.

Would Ireland retain its present position in making EU laws vis-à-vis the other countries?

No. Absolutely not. Under Lisbon more power would be transferred to the political elites (not the citizens) of the biggest states of all, Germany, France, Italy and the United Kingdom. So the Lisbon Constitution would radically change the balance of power. The small states would get weaker and more marginal, the big states would, metaphorically if not actually, get bigger: their political elites would become more powerful.

Q: Is this a matter of voting strengths?

Yes, of course it is, especially for political elites. And the arithmetic of it is important. When Ireland joined the then EEC on 1 January 1973 we had three votes against 10 each for Germany, Britain, France and Italy. The biggest states had over three times more voting power than we did. In 2001 under Nice this went up and the four biggest Member States gained four times our strength. They had 29 votes against our seven votes. That was considered fair enough because the four big Member States each lost a Commissioner under Nice. They used to have two each. This was reduced to one – although Tanaiste Mary Coughlan still thought Member States had two when she was on a radio debate with me during the Lisbon campaign.

Does the voting situation get better or worse under the Lisbon Treaty?

Under the Lisbon Constitution the political elites of Germany would have 20 times more influence than Ireland in the Council because voting will be based primarily on population size. We do not expect this to lead to a steam-rolling through of legislation. It will be more subtle than that. But even so, when we look at it – on any terms – it is not fair to surrender or pool so much power while massively reducing our voting weight. Such a transaction is unconscionable. This would be patently absurd. Whoever actually negotiated this deal for Ireland – all of them – should be fired as incompetent or worse.

How did you discover this set of voting circumstances?

The figures are right there in the draft Constitution and the Lisbon Treaty. They are not easy to find but they would become very important. They are difficult to use and to remember. And of course, because populations change, they also change every year.

Is this another secret strategy?

Specifics in treaties are often hard to find. There is
more to it, however. There is a voting requirement in
Lisbon where a majority of Member States have to be
behind all laws as well. To be more precise: 55% of
Member States must vote in favour of a law, according to
the Lisbon Treaty. This majority also has to represent
states with 65% of all EU citizens. It is this 65% rule that
will move power from the many small states to the few big
Member States. If you were to add Turkey, with a population of almost 72 million into the mix, which would have
grown to nearly 100 million when it actually joins the
Union – something our Government supports – the num-
bers start to look really nuts.

Are you saying the small states – including Ireland – will lose out under the Lisbon voting system?

Categorically, yes. As a result of this part of the Lisbon
Treaty, 15 Member States can vote down 12 Member
States as long as the 15 between them have 65% of the
total EU population. In an enlarged EU, with 32 Member
States, 17 countries can in effect vote down the National
Parliaments of 15 countries in one vote. This is not a
healthy or democratic way of taking decisions. Small
Member States will inevitably be marginalised. The bigger
states will not need to listen to their arguments as they did
in the past.

The proposed new system runs the risk of making the
Union very unpopular with the citizens of most states and
with National Parliaments, particularly when Member
States are voted down in too many sensitive areas, which
inevitably would end up happening. This could bring the
Union down a slippery slope towards break-up and that
would be a disaster. The trigger-mechanism for the break-

up is introduced by the Lisbon Treaty. It is called Article 50, 'The Withdrawal from the Union Clause'.

What is your solution?

Libertas proposes a much more balanced way of making decisions. We would also allow most decisions to be decided by majority vote, but we would require 75% of Member States to be behind all European laws, as against the half of them that are needed to make up the necessary number of weighted votes today, or the 55% of them laid down by the Lisbon Constitution. This would mean there would be far more support for EU laws among the Member States, both big and small, and it would mean that the number of States in favour of a law would represent the great majority of people of the Union.

The EU's voting rules are presently very confusing. Even specialist journalists covering the decision-making process in Brussels sometimes don't know how many votes their own country possesses in the Council, although I suspect that will change once your book comes out. This is how complicated it has all become.

This is the reality: the EU is governed in secret by a voting system only few people have heard about and no one can remember. That is a truly alarming and stupid situation, except, possibly, for those elites who do understand how to use it and are therefore in a privileged position. It has to change.

Again, the question is obvious: what will you do about it?

Libertas will advocate making it much simpler. First, we will campaign to give each Member State one single vote, independent of size, in the Council. Then we will require that the 75% majority of Member States also represents the majority of EU citizens.

Are there guidelines from outside the EU?

Recent changes in the United States have made Europeans look with greater interest at that country, with an increased level of questioning about possible parallels that we might follow in Europe. In the American Senate each American state has two senators. This is irrespective of their size. Why can't we do the same? Why can't we treat the European states equally? To borrow a phrase, yes we can... In fact, yes, we must.

This is the normal way of making decisions in international bodies. The thinking behind it, surely, is one of being true to National/Member State sovereignty. Rather than judging power by voting weight, voting on EU laws should not be based on a notion of sovereignty that reflects a biased preference for the bigger countries.

Are there internal European examples to follow?

In the German Bundesrat the biggest German state, North Rhine Westphalia, with 18 million citizens, possesses six votes against three for the smallest German state, Saarland, with one million citizens. In Federal Germany itself, in other words, the biggest Member State only receives twice as many votes as its smallest. Contrast that with the EU proposal under Lisbon: in today's EU, Germany possesses four times Ireland's voting strength. Under the Lisbon Treaty this would increase to 20 times our strength in one single change.

Or looked at another way, Germany's current 29 votes in making EU laws amount to 8% of the total votes on the Council of Ministers. By moving to a population basis for making EU laws under Lisbon, Germany's relative voting strength would more than double to 17%, France's present voting strength of 8% would increase to 13%, Britain's and Italy's current 8% would go to 12% each, while Ireland's voting weight would fall from its present 2% to 0.8%.

That is a dumb deal however you try to dress it up. It is a very major adjustment, not a marginal one. It is a truly massive shift in real power. It is much more drastic than anyone seems to understand or has fully grasped. What I do not understand is this: why has it been accepted by the Irish Government? Why was it accepted by the governments of the other smaller Member States whose voting weight is slashed? How did this happen? Was someone asleep at the wheel? It certainly looks like it, but of course these are the same people who say 'yes' to everything. The negotiators on the opposite side must have been rolling around in stitches laughing at them. It's the consequence of mediocrity and low expectations.

What real effect will the Lisbon voting changes have?

As the real advantages to the elites – not the citizens – of large states emerge and they are seen to be running the whole show, it will divide Europe. It is also a bad outcome for the citizens of the larger Member States, such as Germany, France, the UK, and Italy because their political elites gain much power but without the corresponding democratic accountability. They can then more easily use Brussels to exercise power and push through policy that would be unacceptable if initiated at home. I call this the 'blame Brussels' clause, whereby elites pursue their policy agendas and say, 'Brussels made us do it.'

What would you seek to do to change it?

Libertas proposes that countries representing the majority of citizens in the whole EU can block any proposal even if the proposal has received the support of 75% of the

Member States. This proposal is much better and it's commonsense. It would unite citizens behind EU decisions. It would make the EU more responsible to the public will. It would make the political activity involved more relevant.

The Libertas proposal creates something that is a much better balance between small and large Member States. It is undoubtedly a more democratic solution, as the Lisbon Treaty has raised serious and legitimate doubts about democracy. People respect political constructions that allow for compromises. People can live with that.

What about the European Parliament? What is the situation there? Surely, if we are talking about democracy, that has to be a vital part of it?

We have plans there. In fact, they are the core focus of our plans. There has to be more involvement in the lawmaking process. Making laws is not new to elected politicians. Most of them in Brussels have experience of making laws elsewhere. They are trained to it and then they find that democratic law-making is not available at the EU level. Libertas will change that.

How will you do it?

It will require a majority from the European Parliament to vote through all laws. In the European Parliament under the Lisbon Treaty Germany would have 96 seats against only 12 from Ireland. Here, in the second chamber, the same unfairness and inequity is reflected in what happens. There is a big difference between Member States according to their size and it has to be made more even and fairer. When Ireland joined the EU Germany had 36 seats against 10 to Ireland. They had 3.6 times our number of seats. Now they will have eight times our number of seats.

I have accepted previous changes as the fair and reasonable price to be paid for EU enlargement. These have included going from 15 Irish seats to 13 today and 12 for the up-coming election. We have all gone along with these changes in previous treaties to accommodate more Member States. But 12 has to be the bottom line if parties like the Labour Party and Sinn Fein are to have any chance of being properly represented in the Parliament. These are not my parties, but they should have an opportunity to be represented.

Is this the main purpose of Libertas? Are you angry about the democratic unfairness?

It's not anger, not at all, it is business logic. It is an argument about the huge difference between the way Member States apply democratic principles and the critical absence of the same principles in the operation of the European Union.

With the operation of Libertas, is it both fact-giving and fact-finding?

You could say that. Once people understand these things, they are surprised that the majority are not more angry. To be outraged by something you have to know about it first. It's a bit like this: to be angry at someone who has run over your dog, you first of all need to know your dog has been run over and you need to know that you had a dog in the first place. People just don't know. I have got over the outrage and want argument about our future to be true to the facts and that people should know what the facts are. If people then choose to give up their freedom, they have made an informed choice. I have never said this before, but I'm quite sure that if most of the voters that voted Yes to Lisbon knew the facts of what was in the Treaty they would have voted No.

Why would any informed voter support a Treaty giving the elites of the biggest Member States more power in both law-making chambers and giving vastly more power to unelected, unknown bureaucrats? It is not fair or decent. Fairness is a condition for popular support for the Union. Fairness has always underpinned democracy, ever since Charles I defied his own Parliament, ever since the people of Boston threw their over-taxed tea into the harbour and said, 'No taxation without representation.' It has been the same with us. Ireland won her independence on the same grounds: that the people govern themselves and hold accountable those who make their laws.

The Libertas proposal is fairer; in fact, its fairness is so obvious that it cannot be credibly argued against. That's why the attacks against Libertas have been so vicious – they just can't defeat our argument. It's like arguing against the need for daylight.

Do you think Member States should still retain a veto?

In the Libertas proposal we have also inserted a right for Member States to raise a veto on very sensitive issues in the European Council meetings. We have taken the proposal from Jean Monnet's right-hand man, his advisor, Georges Berthoin, who proposed to offer every Prime Minister a right to raise a veto in a meeting of the European Prime Ministers. In this way very sensitive questions would find unanimous agreement.

This would happen at the Summit Meetings. This would mean political power would operate at the highest level. By allowing that, one would avoid a range of blocking episodes on minor questions not important enough to be raised by the Prime Ministers.

What else do you demand?

These are democratic proposals, not demands. Libertas has proposed a further safety valve by allowing a majority in the National Parliaments to instruct their Prime Ministers to raise a veto on vital issues.

I believe this to be the best possible compromise between efficiency in making EU laws through majority votes, respect for National Parliaments and finally respect for voters in each Member State. Our proposal for reformed decision-making and law-making methods in the Council has big advantages. It is easy to learn. It is easy to remember. And this applies not only to Ministers, but to the media and voters as well. We may then be able to read in the newspapers how a European law was passed, by whom, and for what purpose.

What is wrong with the European Parliament? Can its operation be improved? What are the practical requirements?

The European Parliament is simply not run as an efficient entity. Nor is it a real Parliament! The word does have an important meaning. In normal democratic states 'Parliament' is the name for the institution that decides our laws and appoints and controls the government. In the EU the legislative power is – as I have explained – divided between the non-elected Commission and the Council of Ministers, which is far away from us and impossible to control.

How bad is the EU democratic problem?

I think it is very bad indeed. And I think nothing to change it has been proposed in the attempts by the Irish Minister for Foreign Affairs, Micheál Martin, and the Junior Minister for Europe, Dick Roche, as well as the

Taoiseach, at the December 2008 Summit. Seemingly, they did not reckon with the EU's fundamental democratic shortcomings. As I have said, these are serious. Probably, they realized that no one was going to change the concentration of power in the hands of non-elected structures without a fight. They had no stomach for a fight with Brussels' elites. They decided it would be easier to turn and fight their fellow Irish citizens, a very Irish solution.

Is that the real core of the problem? That we are locked into a form of frozen submission to the will of the European majority?

It is bad that the core of EU law-making is secret. We have secret meetings in this secret government of the non-elected, operating through non-accountable ambassadors and their many helpers. We have the European Council and the European Commission operating through literally thousands of secret working groups. This is not just bad, it is quite unacceptable.

Why does the Parliament not make more of a fuss about this?

It has accepted the system. It has become part of the system. The European Parliament is content to look as if it works like a real Parliament. It does not, but when this point is raised its members look the other way. They have not got the powers of a normal Parliament, and we should all be disturbed by that. But the members do not complain, nor do the Ministers or Heads of Government. It is all a wrong-headed but convenient charade. The Parliament has no say in anything that is really important in the execution of power.

What are your specific criticisms?

These are the things that worry me. It is the Prime Ministers in a secret summit meeting in the European Council who appoint all the Commissioners. The European Parliament can reject their choice of a full Commissioner list but they cannot elect another Commission.

The European Parliament may vote on the proposed EU laws according to their own rules but the votes are artificial, they do not count fundamentally. The Council of Ministers – or in practice their civil servants – fundamentally decide the laws. That is how it is now. That is how it works with the present Nice Treaty. That is how it will be under the Lisbon Treaty and its new Constitution for the EU. They are identical. It has been bad in the past and it will get worse.

But surely the European Parliament speaks out? Surely it has a role? We certainly hear from its members? How do you explain that?

The lack of formal power does not hinder the elected MEPs from having a real impact on many European laws. This is a paradox, difficult but important to understand. MEPs cannot propose laws. That is the truth. But they can propose amendments to the proposals from the Commission. If the Commission accepts an amendment it can only be rejected in the Council if all representatives decide something different unanimously. It is an important but limited expression of power.

The European Parliament can also reject a proposed law by an absolute majority of its members. This threat can make both the Council and the Commission listen to the Parliament's views. But why should the Parliament use an absolute majority when the Council and the Commission operate on the basis of either a weighted or a simple majority?

MEPs are efficient in using the opportunities they have. The European Parliament has gained a lot of real influence over the years. That is true and is really an endorsement of all the things I say about democracy. People who are elected do have a natural and inalienable mandate of some kind and it badly needs to be strengthened. At present, though it cannot be called real legislative power. I have met active MEPs who had a bigger influence on certain laws than many Ministers and members of National Parliaments, although they do not initiate or really decide them! This is the positive side of the Parliament we seldom hear about and it is here that Libertas sees a potential to be effective.

How does the European Parliament deal with the vast amount of material going through the Commission, the Council, the offices?

The European Parliament is quite well organized. It has sectoral committees that elect rapporteurs to follow the negotiations on any directive. They also coordinate their position with coordinators from the different political groups.

MEPs have no right to receive the relevant updated legislative documents from the Commission and Council services. That is in clear breach of the kind of transparency that is needed. The whole system is full of democratic deficits of this kind. Even so, the smarter among the MEPs find their ways through private or political channels. They are also served by busy lobbyists. Sometimes the lobbyists have the documents that are not sent to the Parliament. In other words, according to what I have been told by different insiders, a workable system of sorts has developed.

Does this make you favour the European Parliament?

Well, although the weakest, Parliament is the most democratic of all the European institutions. Libertas does not underestimate the possible real influence of our MEPs – if we are elected.

The Lisbon Treaty will increase the areas of so-called common decision-making where the European Parliament can reject a proposal or propose an amendment to a Commission draft law. In 19 policy areas this is a progressive step which is also supported by Libertas.

But in 49 areas the National Parliaments lose much more power than is gained by the European Parliament. Therefore the overall result is negative from a democratic point of view. Voters and National Parliaments are the losers. The democratic deficit will grow under Lisbon.

The legislative function of the National Parliaments is primarily moved to the executive in the EU. What is termed 'co-decision' for the European Parliament is only a veneer. This procedure offers the active MEPs real influence but not real legislative power where it is a simple majority in the European Parliament that adopts every law as in the National Parliaments.

Libertas proposes that every single European law has to be positively approved by a normal majority in the European Parliament. Why should this be so difficult to attain? After all, this is what we practice in each National Parliament more or less all the time?

3

THE PARLIAMENT AND HOW IT WORKS

How do you judge the impact of the Lisbon Treaty on the European Parliament?

I can easily understand how, in general, most members of the European Parliament are happy with the Lisbon Constitution. They will certainly have some increased areas of influence. But there is something wrong in this. Their relatively minor gains, in Brussels and Strasbourg, are at the expense of huge losses by their own National Parliaments. Why is the big change of power from the National Parliaments supported by the TDs and MPs who lose the legislative power that is delegated to them by their own Constitution? Does it mean that parliamentarians, who should be reflecting the public will, are becoming part of the hidden system? Or are they just unaware?

This is why 90% of French MPs voted in favour of the proposed EU Constitution. At the same time, 55% of French voters voted against it for the very simple, democratic reason that they would lose the final word on a lot of laws binding on them. They would lose the possibility of standing for election and then proposing new laws. This is a major point, central to my whole argument: it is that the very core of democracy still does not exist in the EU.

How difficult is it all? Does it have to be complicated?

The so-called 'co-decision' for the European Parliament has different phases. First the Commission proposes a draft. It is then sent for readings in the Council of Ministers and the European Parliament.

In its first reading the Parliament can propose amendments by a normal majority of voting members. The non-elected Commission then decides on the amendments from the elected MEPs. If the Commission says OK the amendment can be approved by a qualified majority in the Council, which is 255 out of 345 possible votes.

And if the Council says no?

If the Council does not accept the proposed amendment it is automatically rejected. The European Parliament can make a second try in a second reading. In the second reading the Parliament has to assemble an absolute majority of its members behind all amendments.

Today this means that 393 members must vote in favour. If an amendment is supported by 392 votes against none the President of the Parliament has to conclude: 'Sorry – your amendment has failed.'

It seems democracy is weighted against the Parliament.

Heavily. If all members of the European Parliament took part in all votes this would not be a big problem. But there are always more than 100 members who do not take part in a vote. So, in reality, amendments can only be carried if both sides of the Parliament vote in favour.

Amendments need to be approved by the two big groups, the Socialists in the PES and the Christian Democrats-Conservatives in the EPP party. It is very difficult to have amendments approved without the support of the majority of members in the two biggest groups.

Is that not the opposite of how democracy works in the Dáil?

Precisely. A tangled web has been woven for European parliamentary success. And even then, if there is an absolute majority of MEPs behind an amendment, it is still not approved! Then the Commission can decide once more whether they support or oppose the proposed amendment.

If the non-elected Commissioners support the amendment it must then be approved by the qualified majority in the Council – 255 out of 345 votes. If the Council does not deliver 255 votes for an amendment they will then call for a third reading in what is called a 'Conciliation Committee'. Here 27 members of the European Parliament will meet with representatives from the Commission and the Council and try to draft a compromise.

This compromise should be approved by 255 votes in the Council of Ministers and a majority in the European Parliament.

If it is complicated for those who run it, how do journalists deal with it? How can they inform the public? Doesn't it make it all completely remote?

There is no doubt that it is a very complicated procedure. It is either impossible to follow for journalists, or they concentrate on some minor aspect of a proposed law that may possibly interest people. In fact, many are concerned more with gossip and alarmist reports about this or that rather than with a conscientious coverage of the Parliament in the work it does do.

It is a strange system, after all. In the light of what I have told you, this is not surprising. The so-called 'Conciliation Committees' meet in secret. The real negotiations never take place there, I have been told. In reality, senior civil servants from the Commission meet the rapporteurs from the Parliament with their staff and staff from the Council and they then find possible compromises between the lot of them.

And what role has the Council of Ministers?

In this phase the Council Presidency normally plays a formal role. The voice of the Member States is weak. The role of the Commission is strong. Even so, in this atmosphere strong and active MEPs can still gain real influence on the final outcome of a law. But many don't try. Many are interested in other things.

And what does Libertas intend?

As for ourselves – and even if it is not a true parliamentary democracy – we will take the European Parliament seriously. We will play our constructive part in the building of the necessary alliances behind amendments that we agree with.

In the end, the basis for parliamentary influence will always be an amendment carried by 393 votes. Every vote counts. That is the reason that MEPs from Libertas will have to be active in their committees and take part in all important legislative votes in the plenary sessions.

The way you talk about the operation of parliamentary democracy makes it seem precarious. Is it that our elected politicians are scared of democracy?

Of course they are! Did you ever see Charles Haughey go confidently to the country on any issue? He was always forced. It's the same with other leaders. And it will always be like that. The same political interests – that are primarily concerned with getting re-elected – operate in Europe.

Are they not also concerned with money? How do you propose to address the greed that is concealed behind the secrecy?

That and corruption are huge problems in the European Union. Libertas members will also publish how they spend assistance allowances paid from the European Parliament to members. There have been many scandals over the years.

In fact, the European Parliament is more famous for its greed for money than for its influence on law-making. The fraudulent members are nowadays a minority but they destroy the image of the whole Parliament. And it still goes on. The European political 'act' has not been cleaned up.

Do we pay too much for this apparent political charade?

From 2009 all members of the European Parliament will have the same salary paid by European tax payers. This monthly salary will be a fixed amount which will be taxed at a specially low rate of EU tax. Member States will then have the possibility of asking members to pay an extra tax so that MEPs can be taxed the same way as the voters in their countries. We would suggest a fixed formula for an MEP's salary tying into the overall economic environment in the EU27 block. For example, 3-3.5 times the three-year average GDP per capita for the EU27 would imply a current salary of €82,000. Fixed to the average level of income in the EU, salaries of MEPs would then reflect both the relative economic performance of the EU as a whole and the relative cost of living in Europe. This in turn will ensure that MEPs are directly aware of the economic conditions their policies foster and the impact these have on European citizens. It will also make MEPs' earnings transparent to the citizens.

What about travel expenses and hiring their own families?

Another scandal is that for many years MEPs have been able to earn an extra tax-free salary from their travel expenses. They were still paid for a business-class ticket even if they travel economy class. This fraudulent system disappears for the new Parliament elected in June 2009. And it is not before time. From this year they will have their travel expenses paid on the basis of their actual costs and we would suggest removing the entitlement to business-class travel for short-haul flights. It is estimated that excessive travel and travel allowances amount to some €15,000 per annum per MEP. We estimate that removing the business-class entitlement alone will save around €5,000 a year for each MEP or up to €4 million altogether.

For many years, MEPs could also pocket an assistance allowance for themselves by hiring family members or friends. This system was revealed in a secret auditing report from the European Parliament showing a lot of fraud. The majority in the European Parliament then decided to keep the report secret from the public. It is still secret. That is a disgrace, one of many.

The scandal resulted in a change in the rules so that the in-coming members could not steal the assistance allowances any longer for the persons they hire in Brussels. These will be paid by the Parliament directly after the elections in June.

But while these measures are obviously commendable, surely it won't completely prevent the culture of dishonesty from continuing?

The MEPs can still misuse money to be spent in the Member States. This is why the Libertas election programme commits its members to publish how they spend their assistance allowance.

For me, it is very difficult to understand why the two biggest groups in the Parliament and the group led by the Irish MEP Brian Crowley (Fianna Fail) can defend the decision not to publish an auditing report showing fraud in the Parliament. What do they want to hide? I suppose the answer is: they can and will defend it. But it is a disgrace.

Has fraud become endemic?

The problem with the majority in the European Parliament is that they have been part of a fraudulent system for so many years. It looks like they still have great difficulty getting rid of the bad habit of earning a lot of money for themselves or their parties.

We know it isn't corrupt but there is a ridiculous waste of money in the Brussels-Luxembourg-Strasbourg circus. What do you think should be done about that?

I have never understood why the members of the European Parliament accept the travelling circus between Brussels, Luxembourg and Strasbourg. There are buildings for the full Parliament in each of these three towns. The European Parliament meets 12 times a year for a week in Strasbourg, and then maybe 10 times with shorter sessions in Brussels. More than 2000 persons are employed to work for the Parliament in one town between Strasbourg and Brussels: Luxembourg.

The extra costs of all this have been estimated as being around €500 million per year for all the institutions. The extra unnecessary production of CO_2 has been estimated to be some 20,000 tonnes per year. A Libertas group in the next Parliament will propose bringing this travelling circus to an end.

What will be your proposal?

We will simply ask the MEPs to vote for one single voting place. After that vote we will propose an indicative vote on where this single voting place should be: Strasbourg or Brussels.

It is then up to the Prime Ministers to amend the existing Treaty protocol on locations for the different institutions. They could also offer compensation to the town that will lose their European Parliament. Perhaps it could become the location of the first of the 'new renaissance universities' Libertas is proposing for Europe. That would be a major boost for the city involved and would be of greater benefit to that region than hosting a part-time Parliament building. Although I do ask myself: why should they? What kind of a parliamentary circus are we running? What do the public think of this nonsense?

But what if this concept is rejected?

If the Prime Ministers refuse to establish one working location, the European Parliament can then adopt – on its own – the annual calendar of meetings, with all major debates entailing votes to take place in the location decided by the indicative vote.

The Prime Ministers will have to accept the result because it is the Parliament's sole right to establish its meeting calendar so long as they respect the formal Treaty commitment regarding the holding of meetings.

You mentioned the environmental price that has to be paid. What do you intend to do about that?

If these changes are made, both the costs and CO_2 emissions should fall dramatically. I cannot see how the European Court would be able to change a calendar decision on what parliamentary topics are debated and voted on where. If the EU Court makes the Parliament's decision invalid, the members have at least done what was possible to do to save taxpayers' money and members' time.

What can be done about parliamentary sessions in different places?

More than one million European citizens have signed a petition to call for one workplace. The two big groups in the European Parliament and the group led by Fianna Fail's Brian Crowley would not even allow the European Parliament to debate this citizens' initiative petition from Europe's citizens. This was the first time European citizens used the mechanism of a citizens' initiative, which was one of the 'positives' that Crowley's party tried to use to promote the Lisbon Treaty! MEPs should have welcomed this first initiative from citizens. It had been the initiative of a special reform group in the European Parliament. Libertas will be pushing a committed agenda for real change and reform in this institution.

Furthermore, the European Parliament needs and deserves a blast of fresh air from a new Libertas party which has not been linked to the existing power-sharing between the two biggest groups and all the other bad habits and corruption of the past.

4

THE EUROPEAN COURT OF JUSTICE

You mention the European Court of Justice. What do you feel about it?

The normal function of a court is to adjudicate on specific cases of conflict. The judges read the law carefully. Eventually they give their written findings. They are obliged – or should be – to give their honest judgment as to what was intended by law-makers. When law-makers in the parliaments of properly functioning democracies think the court has gone too far, or has misjudged their intentions, the elected members of parliament can change the law.

At the same time they cannot change the court's verdict. This is because we also have to respect the division of powers between the legislative, executive and judicial arms of government.

What is so different about the European Court of Justice?

The European Court of Justice in Luxembourg has given itself an entirely different role: they are highly 'activist' judges. They alter and change the law and they even change the basic Treaties on their own. This is an extraordinary departure from accepted practice in most democracies. It's blatant legislating from the court bench and these people are not elected nor democratically accountable.

One of the most stunning facts regarding this so-called

Court – which, remember, is given absolute primacy in the Lisbon Treaty – is that it is not like any court we recognise. Why? Because when you appear before the Irish High Court or Supreme Court you are judged by experienced judges. Now get this: you don't need to have ever been a judge to be appointed to this European Supreme Court. There are people who have sat there and who are sitting there right now legislating and adjudicating from this most senior bench, who have zero previous judicial experience.

Right now, Austrian Socialist MEP Maria Berger is widely expected to be appointed the next Austrian judge at the European Court of Justice. She has no experience of ever having been a judge, not even, as far as I am aware, in a dancing competition. It is amateurs like this that we would place above our laws and Constitution if we agree to the Lisbon Treaty. All European Member States, High Court and Supreme Court Justices should make their own judgments about this. This is not how democracy is supposed to work.

My first surprise with the European Court of Justice was when I heard about a verdict defining abortion as a service under the Internal Market rules in the EU. For example, for most citizens in Ireland abortion is a serious ethical question dealt with by Ireland's Supreme Court and governed by our Constitution.

In the so-called 'Grogan-case' from 1991, the Internal Market rules on free movement of services were simply extended to include abortion. In the outcome the EU Court accepted the Irish restrictions on abortion, but they emphasised that the EU Court was competent in the matter. The Court's Advocate-General had proposed to give Irish women equal access to abortion.

Could the EU Court follow the Advocate-General another day and maybe also include such matters as human cloning and research into animal human hybrids as a simple economic service?

Ireland requested a special protocol where the EU would have to respect the Irish Constitution's rule on abortion. This means that countries without such a protocol may be forced to regard abortion as a normal economic service like hiring a car or buying a book.

So, far-reaching interpretations of existing national law, that were never decided by elected TDs or MPs or the Member State representatives in the Council of Ministers, are being made by this European Court. It's an entirely new departure, from my perspective: a simple but devastating process of non-elected judges making the law rather than interpreting it. Since these EU judges are the interpreters of the basic Treaties, the elected and appointed law-makers have no possibility of changing this system of judicial activism. The elected legislators cannot even pass a law outlawing the effects of a bad 'activist court verdict' for future reference.

How far is all this a departure from the courts in normal democracies?

I regard it as a major abuse of the democratic principles that we cherish in our own country, across the Union, and in the United States, Canada, Australia, India, and many other countries around the world.

The only possibility of changing abortion from being regarded as an economic service to being a moral-ethical question would be to call for an Intergovernmental Conference of the Member States and amend the Treaty by unanimity, followed by ratification by each of the 27 Member State Parliaments. The so-called 'agreement' or guarantee for Ireland on this abortion question reported from the December 2008 Summit does not make sense because it is a complete fudge and is unlikely to withstand a legal test in the European Court.

Have you other examples of damage done by the European Court of Justice?

In December 2007 the EU Court of Justice took another far-reaching decision when the judges made it illegal for trade unions to take industrial action against a foreign company if it paid its workers the minimum wage of the host country but not the national standard wage above the minimum. Before this so-called 'Laval-case' in Sweden Member States could decide their national labour laws on their own. A Member State could insist on respect for national agreements on wages and salaries and uphold national standards negotiated in collective bargaining.

The difference is immense. In Ireland the official minimum wage is €8.65 an hour. The average salary in most occupations is twice this. Because of the Laval case and related EU court judgments it is now legal in European law for a firm to hire cheap labour and put Irish workers on standard wages out of their jobs. I refer you to the notorious Irish Ferries case. That was an example of Irish workers having their jobs undercut by imported labour. It was a telling example.

Has anything been attempted to rectify the Laval Case?

As it happens, yes, and the consequences would have been significant if it had succeeded. Independent MEP Kathy Sinnott drafted a proposal for a legally binding protocol to be attached to the Lisbon Treaty which would set the Laval judgment aside. This was the only possible way to overturn the Court's verdict. The European trade unions made a similar proposal – with no result. Look, I mention these cases as an example of far-reaching decisions being made that are far removed from the democratic process. You may agree or disagree with the Court's decision in this instance, but the dysfunctional model is there and it needs to be fixed.

Where does the present EU Court system lead?

It's clearly ridiculous to give non-elected, inexperienced, sometimes novice judges this kind of power. The Libertas programme would aim to change the Lisbon Treaty's provisions for the European Court of Justice, turning things around so that no inexperienced or politically activist judges will preside. We will seek to ensure that only those who have served as senior judges in the Member States can qualify for a seat on the European Court of Justice.

We also propose to have public hearings on the nomination of new judges and to leave it to the Dáil and the other Member State Parliaments to appoint their next national judge in the European Court. Since the Court makes a lot of decisions that politicians would never take in public, we need to control judicial nominations from the bottom up using the voters' elected representatives.

Today the EU Court works in French. We have no guarantees that an Irish judge will be involved when Irish affairs are being adjudicated on. The deliberations of the Court are secret and the votes of individual judges are unknown. We have a much more open system in Ireland and this should be a universal principle. We don't even know if a verdict in the EU Court of Justice is made by a narrow majority or by unanimous agreement amongst the relevant judges.

You may ask, how do we tolerate this? I'll tell you how:

because people are absolutely unaware of it. I suspect that many of the Lisbon Treaty cheerleaders in parts of the media are also unaware of it. Libertas will change that.

Libertas intends that its programme will be a clean-out of the bad habits of the past. We need a European Court to decide on conflicts between Member States and the European institutions, citizens and businesses. We need a reformed European Court where justice is affordable by ordinary citizens and where capable, experienced judges stick to their defined role as judges with the function of interpreting the law – not making and shaping it.

5

WHY ARE WE RULED BY SO MANY PEOPLE IN BRUSSELS?

Is Europe run by too many people? Is it run by the wrong people? Are we able to change them?

The European Commission employs 30,000 civil servants. This means around 170,000 people if one includes assistants, transport staff, catering staff etc. This is according to a study by the British think-tank, Open Europe. There are 3000 working groups under the Commission. The Commission in turn is divided into Directorates-General for each topic. Each Directorate is headed by a Director-General.

The entire Commission civil service is led by a Secretary-General. At present this important job is held by an Irish civil servant, Catherine Day. For each Department there is a political chief, the Commissioner. The former Maoist Communist and later Portuguese Prime Minister José Barroso is the direct political boss of Catherine Day and between them they direct all the other Departments. Each Commissioner has a personal cabinet with around 20 staff and one or two drivers to help transport them around.

But what about the Commission working groups and the fact that they have been kept secret?

As well as having their personal Cabinets, members of the Commission also run the 3000 secret working groups. This is less well-known. Until 2004 even the list of working groups and the issues they covered were secret. The former leader of the EU-critical group in the European Parliament, Jens-Peter Bonde, had tried for many years to have the list made public. He also tried to get it from various Secretary-Generals. They refused to publish the list.

When Barroso was collecting votes to support his appointment as Commission President in 2004 he made a promise to Bonde to publish the full list. He called on the Secretary-General to hand it over immediately. Next morning Bonde received a list of 3094 Commission working groups. Up to that point their existence had been concealed. The list will shortly be available on the Libertas website (www.libertas.eu).

Barroso also promised to publish the names of the members of the 3000 working groups. Some names have been delivered in a new database from 2009, but the list is still not complete.

The activities of many working groups are still secret – even for elected MEPs and the National Parliaments. The Commission uses the many secret working groups to generate support for their version of more 'integration, harmonization and efficiency'. They often hand-pick people, pay daily allowances and travel expenses for support networks working for the Commission – sometimes when this may be against the wishes of their own National Parliaments. Such working groups do not represent a democratic problem as long as they are manned by civil servants appointed from and representing their Member States. But a lot of members are handpicked because their views are known to be congenial to the Commission's own or because they represent particular, favoured interests. It is a lobbyist's dream.

Can you give an example?

Well, yes, for one, take the advisory group on tobacco. In this working group 12 representatives are from the tobacco growers, six from the tobacco industry, six from the tobacco sales sector and one representative each of the trade unions and the consumers. There is not a single representative from the health authorities. It may be right or wrong, but the composition of every Commission advisory group should be public and transparent. For example, why not broadcast their meetings over the internet for transparency purposes?

Why can't the agendas, the working documents and the minutes be made public? What do they do in our name and for our taxpayers' money that they do not want us to see?

I acknowledge there may be some working groups that may be working on proposals where secrecy may be required. This could be to avoid rumours that might ruin a company or increase the value of other companies. For example, a particular company or special interest group might get significant benefits if they knew that a particular directive was in the pipeline.

With respect to this, Libertas would have a simple solution. The Parliament can simply allow derogations from a normal practice of transparency for special categories of decisions or in particular instances.

Libertas would also propose reducing the number of working groups so that they would only exist for genuine cross-EU issues which the Member States cannot deal with efficiently on their own.The bottom line has to be that the EU must reduce its activities in some areas and focus on achieving excellence in the areas where the Union can make a positive difference.

Is it possible to extrapolate from this the size of the problem? How many laws are we looking at coming from the EU?

The situation facing a lawyer working on EU legal issues, not to mention the ordinary citizen, is a massive one. The European Commission has admitted that there are now more than 20,000 EU laws and more than 100,000 pages of EU legal texts.

There is no single European law book where you can read all the EU laws on any specific topic. The EU does not tell us the number of laws or the number of pages used for publishing them. This is absolutely nuts. I find it bizarre that the Commission requires every sheep farmer to be able to count the number of sheep he has; yet, at the same time, the Commission does not count its own output of laws. There are way too many pages of EU law, many of them frivolous and resulting in unnecessary red tape. Libertas would make it a priority to reduce the number, volume and output of EU laws and red tape.

How do you envisage Libertas doing this?

The first challenge is the way EU laws are prepared. Comprehending the initial text of a newly introduced law is possible, for the simple reason that you can get a readable text. It may be difficult to read but at least it is written in sentences and paragraphs. I don't mean this as a joke. Far from it. But the problems over EU law really begin when the laws are amended. This means a new and separately produced directive or regulation. Suddenly the legal text will read: 'Change 4 for 8 in Article X, etc.' That means another level of documentation that has to be traced and consulted to find out what the law says. How confusing is that? It is only possible for a few highly specialised lawyers to read and understand the actual status of

EU laws after they have been amended and amended again.

This is the reason why the Lisbon Treaty presented such a challenge in terms of comprehending just how bad it is. The Treaty is a classic example of unreadable law. It contains a huge number of proposed Treaty amendments which can only be read and understood if they are inserted in the existing European Treaties. If you only have the amendment to a law can you still read it? Of course not. It is worth noting that the unreadability of the Lisbon Treaty was viewed by many as a triumph in so far as it ensured people would not be able to understand what its effects would be. I quote the Belgian Foreign, Minister Karel de Gucht:

'The Constitutional Treaty was to be more readable. The aim of this Treaty is to be unreadable. The Constitution aimed to be clear, whereas this Treaty had to be unclear. It is a success!' And the former French President, Giscard D'Estang, criticised the Treaty for being presented so that, as he put it: 'Public opinion will be led to adopt, without knowing it, the policies we would never dare present to them directly. All the earlier proposals (from the democratically rejected Constitution) will be in the new text (the Lisbon Treaty) but will be hidden or disguised in some way.'

The Libertas proposal is straightforward: new amendments to EU laws would have to be inserted in the original law. A particular amendment should be written in bold letters when it adds something to the existing text and in italics, with a thin line through it, where a sentence is scrapped.

If it is so simple to do, why haven't they done it?

I don't think anyone expected the need to be able to read the Lisbon Treaty to ever come up. I am pretty sure that those who arranged this thought the Lisbon Treaty would be blindly accepted. There is ample evidence of this kind of thinking. I found all this a startling, even an absurd, demonstration of the arrogance of those proposing the Yes vote. They actually felt that people would trust them and many of them clearly hadn't, and still haven't, the foggiest idea of what they are talking about or proposing. It is this mind-set in some of our politicians today that I find so extraordinarily arrogant...

These politicians chastise the majority of the Irish electorate who made an informed decision on Lisbon. They misled a minority that made an ill-informed decision to vote Yes and while continuing to keep themselves substantially in the dark about the real content of this Treaty, they tell us that we have to vote again. This is so stupid, when you think about it, it almost induces a nosebleed.

Are you saying they were naïve? Or was there a darker desire to obscure the realities of this enormous change?

I will remain as neutral as I can in my answer. I hope that it was ignorance or laziness rather than intent. What I do believe is that this approach emphasizes how the EU is so badly in need of a fresh boost of ordinary, practical, commonsense reality from people who have the capacity to question what they are told in a constructive manner. Libertas policy would work along those lines.

How will this be done?

Libertas will call for all existing EU laws to be consolidated in easy-to-read legal texts for every policy topic and that they should be made available online. We can then just download laws for whatever particular need we have. This will allow citizens to access the law without having to hire a legal specialist for thousands of euro.

Will this make amending the law easier?

It should. At present a huge deal is made about amending European laws. It is deliberately made into a difficult problem. For one thing it always requires the initiative to come from the European Commission. I find it bizarre that no one else can propose an amendment to an existing EU law. If the Commission does not want to amend a law it will simply continue unchanged for eternity – even if every single Member State or a unanimous European Parliament may want a change. That is another of the many denials of democracy.

Are you putting forward the idea of much wider public involvement in EU law-making?

Precisely. And why not? It is the objective of Libertas to make democracy central rather than marginal to the EU. Here again Libertas has another simple solution to the uncontrolled power of the non-elected Commission. And again, it is quite simple: why not add a list of laws to the next Treaty which will disappear automatically after, let us say, eight or 15 years if they are not amended or reviewed before the agreed expiry date? We'll call it the sunset clause. What I'm saying is: give these laws a 'half-life'; then, if they are really needed, they will be reviewed and renewed; if they are not, they will self-delete.

You think that unnecessary EU laws should be allowed to expire?

Yes, absolutely. Isn't the Lisbon Treaty itself, in its actual structure, living evidence of EU laws being changed and updated? This is what has made it such a complicated document. A more radical suggestion would be to let every EU law automatically expire unless it is reformed or at least vigorously scrutinized before a particular date, say 1

January 2015. That way we would force the bureaucrats to propose a Consolidated Readable Version of the laws for their special areas for regular approval.

This would also be helped by adopting the Libertas reform proposal of a necessary 75 per cent support in the Council of Ministers and a normal majority in the European Parliament.

Do you think this is possible?

Yes, in fact it has already happened in another context. On the subject of the Lisbon Treaty, it is interesting to note that in the Convention which drew up the original EU Constitution that is now embodied in Lisbon a consensus of 90 per cent of the Convention members signed a proposal to change the procedures on transparency so that all EU documents and meetings would be public unless special derogations were agreed. Every single member from the 27 Member State National Parliaments – plus Turkey – signed and supported this proposal. All members from the European Parliament – except one French Socialist – supported it. The representatives of 23 governments signed as well. No other single proposal had such substantial support in the Convention. Yet even this sensible proposal did not survive to become part of the draft EU Constitution and it was not inserted in the Lisbon Treaty covert-version of the Constitution.

Why do you think it wasn't implemented?

The EU Prime Ministers simply decided when they signed the Treaty that no European institution should be allowed to publish a Consolidated Readable Version of the Treaties as they would be if amended by Lisbon before that Treaty had been finally approved by all 27 Member States.

Really, you can't make this stuff up. The European Parliament had decided to publish a Consolidated Readable Version, but this decision simply 'disappeared' and was never implemented. The Commission Vice-President responsible for information, Margot Wallström, promised that the Commission would publish a readable version. She was later overruled by President Barroso. He, in turn, was forced to obey the wishes of the Prime Ministers that the document should remain unreadable. Remember what the Belgian Foreign Minister said: '*It is unreadable. It is a success.*'

Did they not also interfere on the issue of holding referendums?

They most certainly did. The Prime Ministers decided to cancel all further referendums on the Lisbon Treaty after the voters' rejection of the first draft Constitution in France and the Netherlands in May and June 2005.

How did we get around that one?

We were the exception forced upon them. Ireland, for its own constitutional reasons, had to have a referendum. It was the only one and no one expected it to 'go wrong'. They presumed that the Irish people would be disinclined or too dumb to scrutinize the Treaty document and challenge the artificial consensus in its favour. They also knew the Irish Government would roll over to have its tummy tickled because with their first-hand experience they knew the Irish Cabinet was staffed with lightweights who would never dare question the people in Brussels whom they saw as their betters. I distributed a Consolidated Readable Lisbon Treaty with a 3000-word alphabetical index before the Irish referendum. It went to journalists and a number of voters. That book was a private initiative from the Foundation for EU Democracy in Brussels, edited by Jens-Peter Bonde. It was quite simple: we wanted people to read the Treaty, the 'Yes' side didn't.

What did Ireland do about that?

The Irish Government simply failed to distribute the text they wanted approved. The Irish Institute for European Affairs printed another consolidated version before the referendum. It was available from the Institute for €25 a copy but had no index.

The Government used millions of euro for state-financed propaganda in favour of the Lisbon Treaty, but failed to publish the text we were voting on. They directly misinformed the public on key contents of the Treaty. I doubt if many of the 'Yes' campaigners ever actually read it, because with rare exceptions they are good people and if they had done their homework and read it, they would have taken another view.

In many of the speeches I made during the campaign, I said that if people didn't listen to a word I had said, they should just read as much of the Treaty as they could bear and then they would know how to vote. The fact is that most 'Yes' voters hadn't a clue about what was actually in the Treaty. They thought they were voting for or against Europe because the 'Yes' side ran an utterly dishonest campaign with sycophantic support from some sections of the media – most especially *The Irish Times*.

What about the Referendum Commission's role in the Lisbon referendum?

The Referendum Commission is supposed to inform voters how the proposed Constitutional Amendment they are being asked to approve to enable Ireland to ratify Lisbon would affect our Constitution. The Dáil voted it €5 million for that purpose and in my opinion the Commission did a poor job of it.

I would say indeed that the Referendum Commission failed completely to spell out the constitutional effects of the Lisbon Treaty. For example, it did not tell people that Lisbon would set up a constitutionally new European Union and would give it its own Constitution which would be made superior to the Irish Constitution if Lisbon was ratified.

Nor did it spell out the implications of us all being given an 'additional' citizenship by the Lisbon Treaty and what the rights and duties of being a citizen of the post-Lisbon EU would entail in addition to the rights and duties of being an Irish citizen. It did not tell us what are the implications of making the EU Charter of Fundamental Rights legally binding for EU citizens. It did not mention that Lisbon would abolish the European Community which we joined in 1973 and which is referred to in the Irish Constitution.

Are you saying the Referendum Commission was one-sided in its approach?

The Referendum Commission confined itself to outlining the less constitutionally important aspects of Lisbon based on the one-sided summaries of the Treaty that Junior Minister Dick Roche and the Department of Foreign Affairs had put out. Even there it omitted important points. For example, it ignored completely the fact that Lisbon would take away from Ireland and the other Member States the right to decide who their national Commissioner would be and would replace that by a right to make 'suggestions' only for the new Commission President to decide. It played down how Lisbon would increase the voting power of the big States in making EU laws by 50% or more, while it would halve Ireland's voting weight.

I recognise that the Referendum Commission was called into being only shortly before the referendum and that it may not have had enough time to get really on top of the Treaty, which is certainly complex. But they have plenty of time now and, if the Government is re-running the same Treaty to get a different result, let us hope the Referendum Commission does a better job next time around.

What about referendum spending generally and the regulatory role of the Standards in Public Office Commission?

It is a real pity the Government took away from the Referendum Commission the job of giving voters the main arguments for and against in Irish referendums. They did that for a specific reason: to get the Nice Treaty through the second time around. This is no way to make or amend laws.

When public money was behind both sides of the argument, private spending was much more limited. The result was that in last year's Lisbon Referendum I calculate the Yes-side outspent the No-side by a factor of four or five to one. That is, if one takes into account spending by the main political parties, which were all on the Yes side, the spending by MEPs and the European Political Groups they belong to, which put out mostly Yes-side material, and pro-Lisbon spending by bodies like IBEC, the IFA, Chambers of Commerce and some of the Trade Unions.

Was all this regulated? Was it under the supervision of the Standards in Public Office Commission?

No. The Standards in Public Office Commission, or

SIPO, takes a very narrow view of what it calls 'third parties' that get involved in referendum campaigning. Anyone who accepts a donation of €127 or over must register with SIPO as a third party and open a political donations bank account. Yet the way the regulation is designed, SIPO has to ignore spending by TDs, MEPs and the European Political Groups which MEPs belong to, and they were heavily involved last year.

It also ignores referendum spending by IBEC and others as long as they use their own resources and do not look for donations as Libertas has done. SIPO has even questioned Libertas for giving out free copies of the Lisbon Treaty which we got from Brussels. Yet this text was totally neutral in content and could have been given out equally freely by the Yes-side groups.

It all sounds very one-sided. Will the EU Commission be taking part in the next referendum?

A very alarming recent development is precisely that. The EU Commission in Brussels, with its limitless resources, is now weighing in on the Yes-side in the lead-in to the referendum re-run through its Dublin office. The EU Commission stands to gain huge new powers under Lisbon. For example, the Lisbon Treaty would give the EU Commission the exclusive right of proposing European laws in something like 30 new policy areas.

So the Commission plans to spend some €2 million over the coming months on an advertising campaign in Ireland to influence opinion in favour of the Lisbon Treaty. This is directed at women and young people in particular, for they strongly rejected Lisbon last year. Yet the EU Commission has no part to play in the ratification of EU Treaties, which are exclusively a matter for the Member States. The Commission has functions in relation to

Treaties after they have been ratified, but not before. Such interference by Brussels in Ireland's referendum is very likely in breach of EU law. It could be in breach of Irish law too, for some of this advertising spending will be indirectly paid for by Irish taxpayers.

Think of it: here is an outside body headquartered in Brussels spending EU taxpayers' money to try to influence Irish voters to approve a Treaty which would give the Commission itself more power and which would reduce the power of the Irish Dáil and of the Irish citizens who elect the Dáil. Few things could be more outrageously undemocratic, yet how many among our politicians and media are outraged by it?

How can this Lisbon Treaty mess be rectified to the benefit of all 27 EU nations?

We have got to make this a much more straightforward, up-front and honest Treaty/Constitution for the European Union. Rule number one should be that it should not exceed 25 pages. That this is an achievable task has already been demonstrated by the likes of the draft Treaty published by *The Economist*.

I have also read a recent draft in Jens-Peter Bonde's book, *From EU Constitution to Lisbon Treaty*. This draft only contains 47 short articles and can be printed on one page of a broadsheet newspaper. I am not at all saying that these drafts are akin to what should be adopted, but these two attempts prove that it is possible to write a very short Constitution or basic Treaty containing all the necessary rules on how to decide laws and respect fundamental rights in the EU. If you print off the US Constitution, it runs to about 13 A4 pages and it seems to have worked fairly well for them for the past couple of hundred years.

What is the difference between this and debating the whole Lisbon Treaty?

The one is possible, the other is impossible. One of the main problems during the referendum was one of incomprehensibility. Ulick McEvaddy hit the nail on the head when he called the text 'unintelligible drivel' and 'gobbledygook'. The problem was further compounded by what was buried in the drivel. A Constitution or a fundamental Treaty should never include the content of laws to be decided but only the rules on how to make and amend those laws. If Member States prefer to continue to have some of the many existing Treaty obligations legally binding at Treaty level, they can then add them in the form of Protocols dealing with specific Treaty Articles from the past.

Are you saying that we need to start again?

I think starting again would be far better than the nonsense that is being pursued, a kind of patch-up solution through Protocols added to the Treaties. This means that an already incomprehensible document, a fundamentally bad design, is going to be made even more ridiculous. I repeat: the important thing is to have a basic Treaty/Constitution which can be read and understood by anyone over the age of 15.

We have to remember, the original Lisbon Treaty was not read by any of the 27 Prime Ministers before they signed it, and that is an indictment of them. This was the result of a collective cave-in to peer pressure. If even one or two of them had had the courage to read the Treaty, ask the questions, take a stand for the truth, others would have followed. This was one of the many pieces of evidence that have led me to the conclusion that Europe is currently afflicted by a tyranny of mediocrity and low expectations, which ends up manifesting itself in constantly underestimating voters, with a resultant loss of the people's trust.

Let us get this right: did no Prime Minister read the Lisbon Treaty?

That is correct. Think about it: not one single Prime Minister had read the Lisbon Treaty text when they signed it on behalf of their nations. Although it was not Brian Cowen who signed for Ireland, when he later became Taoiseach he admitted publicly that he hadn't read it cover to cover. He said more recently that you did not need to read it in order to know what was in it. Was he relying on someone who said to him: 'It's all right. It has been read for you.' Was that the basis on which he campaigned, asking the country to vote Yes? He said later, you did not need to read *Oliver Twist* to know what was in it! Brian became a less than 'Artful Dodger'.

What about the ordinary people?

If it were not so critically important one could forgive politicians for not reading it. But the Prime Ministers deliberately worked on the basis that no one else would get to read it. That is unforgivable. Those Heads of State or Heads of Government did not want the text to be read by their citizens before it had been ratified by all their National Parliaments.

How big was the Lisbon Treaty and Constitution?

The first draft Constitution contained 560 pages. French President Nicolas Sarkozy won the presidential election in France by promising to scrap this over-complicated Constitution and replace it with what he called a 'mini-Treaty'. When the negotiations were finished they found that the new Treaty contained an additional 7229 words.

The Council secretariat was ordered to make the type-font smaller so that more words could be squeezed onto each page. They came up with a different solution. They kept the font the same size but closed the line-spacing, cramming the 7229 words onto 55 fewer pages.

Voila! C'est tres simple. Miniaturisation in action. Thus you make what Sarkozy called a 'mini-Treaty'. The French President also stated that the original Lisbon Treaty would have been rejected by other Member States if their people had been given the opportunity of voting on it. In a meeting in the French Embassy in Dublin last July, President Sarkozy told me that the French people would vote No to the Lisbon Treaty if they had a vote. That is how cynical the whole process has become.

If you are elected to the European Parliament what would be your first course of action with regard to the Treaty?

If Libertas has a sufficient mandate, we will do everything in our power and will work with anyone necessary to establish a short, commonsense, fundamental Treaty/Constitution of 25 pages or so.

This draft – which will emphasise Democracy, Accountability and Transparency – should then be submitted to referendums on the same day in all EU Member States. And let the people have their say, debate it and hopefully get behind it.

I have faith and complete confidence in the people of Europe to make the right decision. Under these circumstances I would be one of those leading the charge for a 'Yes' vote. The result would then have to be ratified by all the National Parliaments and, by the way, if the people say No, then it should be back to the drawing board, because that's democracy.

Do you believe a more transparent Treaty would actually be ratified in all Member States?

I am confident that a basic Treaty or Constitution on these lines would be supported by the vast majority of voters in each Member State. I haven't been overly surprised to find how much we, living in Europe, all think the same way.

Instead of forcing the Irish to vote on the same Treaty twice it would be far better and more democratic to have one referendum in each Member State. It would be by far the best way to have these referendums on a properly democratic Treaty/Constitution where we can expect an enthusiastic Yes from voters in all Member States. A new Treaty/Constitution should contain the key reforms of democracy, accountability and transparency. This would have the effect of giving Europe back to the people. It would make democracy its foundation, it would engage their energy and be a new dawn for the people of Europe.

Can you explain your concept of 'Democracy, Accountability and Transparency'?

By democracy I simply mean that every law should be decided by the voters. It can be done directly in referendums, or by members of parliaments. By accountability I mean that all Commissioners and law-makers should be accountable to voters at the next polling-day or election. By transparency I mean that all law-making should be done in public unless there are compelling reasons to make an exception. Why would anybody be against such straightforward democratic reforms? We need a strong vote for Libertas to insist on 'Democracy', 'Accountability' and 'Transparency'.

6

INVOLVEMENT IN THE EU

How do you envisage ordinary citizens becoming more involved in the European Union?

Libertas wants to promote a more decentralised way of taking decisions. It must be closer to the people of Europe. We prefer decisions to be taken, if you will, bottom-up instead of top-down. In EU language this approach is called 'subsidiarity'. By this word one means that decisions should only be taken at a higher level if that is appropriate and necessary, as it often is; or when it offers extra advantages to the citizens rather than to the ruling elites.

Where did 'subsidiarity' come from?

The principle of subsidiarity was inserted by the 1992 Maastricht Treaty. Since 2006 the European Commission has sent all proposals for new laws to the National Parliaments inviting them to assess them in terms of subsidiarity. In the first 15 months the Commission received 152 evaluations from all the National Parliaments. Not one of them led to a change in a single proposal.

We are getting the distinct impression here of bureaucratic red tape and sheer laziness when it comes to Government participation and diligence in the EU. Would you agree with that assessment?

Members of the National Parliaments do not appear to take their work seriously. They simply accept that civil servants from the Government Departments should some-how determine our views – without us knowing it. This is wrong.

Libertas believes that all proposals for new EU laws should be dealt with in the relevant committee in each National Parliament – like in the Dáil's European Affairs Committee – and eventually in a full session of the Dáil for important proposals. Irish citizens should be informed about new proposals before the negotiations on them start in Brussels. Then we can have our input and possible influence as voters and the media can play their essential role.

And if this doesn't happen?

Then it's a travesty of democracy. It must be challenged. It is becoming apparent that democracy is in crisis in many places, from South and Central America to Europe. It should make us all uncomfortable that this year there are two places in the world where referendums are being repeated because the people gave the 'wrong' answer the first time around. One is Hugo Chavez's Venezuela, the other is Ireland. And the pathetic thing is that at least Ireland had a vote, which is more than can be said for the other 26 Member States of the European Union.

Where should the line be drawn between the EU and the National Parliament, in our case the Dáil?

It is a key question. It was totally avoided during the referendum campaign. The constitutional question was ignored. This issue of where is the heart of our democracy was also ignored. It was kept off the agenda by everyone except ourselves. The fact is, it's up to the people to decide.

On the question of drawing any kind of line between the national level and the EU level, the National

Parliaments could be involved in the adoption of the annual legislative programme of the EU. Representatives from the National Parliaments should meet and formally adopt this legislative programme.

For each topic they should then adopt the legal base for the proposal and thereby decide whether they want binding EU legislation with primacy over national law – or do they just want voluntary coordination, and then leave it to the National Parliaments to decide the law? If you think about it, this is a radical proposal. It is simply not possible under the Lisbon Treaty and we shall all be locked out of going the reform route in the future if we adopt the Lisbon Treaty.

How do you see this 'bottom-up' procedure you speak of actually making a difference?

This bottom-up procedure could change a lot in EU decision-making and give people confidence in the result. The members of our own Dáil would have had their say. Voters could always consult the minutes and electronic votes on a Dáil website and see who voted for or against an EU-related proposal. At polling day we could then either punish or re-elect the members of our National Parliament for how they deal with European legislation.

Libertas will be a strong voice for real subsidiarity. Its approach, if adopted, will bring vivid local and national democracy. It will also insist on accountability and transparency. There are times when the laws ought to be made at EU level, because joint legislation in some particular area will give us a better result than what we could attain at local or national level. Nevertheless all laws, whether European or national, would have to start here, with us.

How much law is coming from Brussels?

The German Ministry of Justice has calculated that 84% of all German laws now originate in the EU. This dramatic figure was brought to public attention by the former German President, Dr Roman Herzog, in *Welt Am Sonntag* in 2007. The German local states have seen that more than half their state legislation is now controlled from Brussels. Brussels not only takes over national parliamentary democracy – it also undermines local democracy. Germany is very sensitive towards centralization in Brussels because Germany itself is a Federation. Germany has 16 'states' or 'Lander' which divide responsibility between the State and Federal governments.

I should also point out that Herzog is former President of the German Constitutional Court in Karlsruhe and he presided over the so-called Charter Convention which drew up the EU Charter of Fundamental Rights. This Court is currently considering a challenge to Lisbon brought by, amongst others, a member of the Von Stauffenberg family, the son of the brave man who tried to assassinate Hitler in his bunker in 1944 and save Germany and the victims of Nazism.

The Charter of Fundamental Rights is now being made part of the Lisbon Constitution as legally binding rules. Herzog criticizes the lack of democracy in EU decision-making the same way as I do now in this interview. He concludes that Germany can hardly be called a parliamentary democracy because of the democratic deficit in the EU. The same point can be made about the other EU Member States.

Herzog has proposed a special 'Subsidiarity Court' to decide on conflicts of power and Treaty interpretation between the Member States and the European institutions. This is a very good proposal and Libertas will include President Herzog's idea in our election programme.

It sounds as if Libertas is fundamentally about putting people first? Might not that be a good slogan to use?

When we started working on the first draft of the Libertas election campaign we considered using the motto 'Put People First', because this was – and is – our intention. In the meantime, the Socialists in Europe, the PES, used the title 'People First' for their election manifesto, which is a little ironic coming from them. I don't think the EU Socialist and Social Democratic parties have lived up to their slogan about putting people first. Libertas will have more creative slogans, although sloganeering isn't really central to our theme. We have got to change the bad habits of Brussels and bring democracy to the heart of the European Union.

What bad habits are you referring to?

There is no tradition of having a neutral and professional staff in the European Parliament. In the European Parliament the Socialist group, the PES, often vote with the so-called Christian-Democrats and Conservatives in the EPP party. They often take joint responsibility for amendments. They elect a Socialist to be the President of the Parliament for the first two-and-a-half-years. Then they jointly elect a so-called 'Christian Democrat' for the remaining two-and-a-half years. In the current European Parliament period a Spanish socialist presided for the first two-and-a-half-years. Now the president of the Parliament is Hans-Gert Pöttering, a German CDU member and former head of the EPP group. Suffice it to say that he has been a big disappointment.

The two big parties control almost two-thirds of the seats, which I believe is 505 out of 785. They also divide the European Parliament's official staff posts between them. For the appointment of higher officers they simply recruit from the staff of their political groups. For that reason all high positions in the Parliament's administration – except one – are from the political groups. They may or may not be properly qualified, but they do not get their jobs because of their qualifications but because they are appointed by the bureaus of the leading political parties. It is a classic example of 'jobs for the boys'.

7

THE FINANCIAL CRISIS

As an entrepreneur, what is your assessment of the financial crisis facing us, particularly in Ireland?

We are possibly in our worst financial crisis since the 1930s. It is a tough thing to say, but true: many families have been encouraged and lured into indebtedness and the political class – both the Government, the Opposition, plus Brussels – have a lot to answer for. The reason they have a lot to answer for is that they failed in their duty to act and sound the alarm when hyperinflation of housing, land and property prices was rampant in the early 2000s. They said and did nothing.

Inflated prices in housing were caused by Government policies in Europe, in Ireland and in the USA. A huge bubble was allowed to develop in the property sector, which tilted whole economies out of balance. The Government and the Banks permitted debt and mortgages that were unsustainable by any sensible risk measure. Property prices soared in line with how much people were able to borrow. There was literally so much money available at such low rates of interest that the tap was gushing out of control. In my small way I tried to draw attention to this in a speech at NUI Galway a few years ago, but no one was listening apart from a few in the crowd.

When housing prices fell dramatically last year the Government had already lost control. The bankers, financial institutions and politicians have impoverished numerous individuals and families by mismanagement of the economy and the money supply. If you were to talk to anyone that approached me for very informal, friendly advice on an investment over the past six or seven years, they would tell you that my advice was not to buy property, but to rent and wait for the inevitable collapse. Frankly, I'm just surprised it did not happen sooner. When I took questions after that speech of mine at NUI Galway, the advice I gave was for investors to go short on Irish property and Banks. I hope some of those listening took some notice and made a few quid.

How in your view have our politicians handled the financial crisis? Did they listen to the many serious warnings from economists and commentators? Did they take heed, for example, of what was appearing in the *Financial Times*? That paper forewarned us all about the impending crisis while our Government sat idly by. Surely they should have been more proactive? Did they react in the good times with the right measures when they first saw the danger signals?

The Government argues that the economic crisis we're facing was unforeseeable. Utter baloney. The clear warnings were there. The Government and the Opposition quite irresponsibly believed in ever-increasing house and property prices, ever-increasing stamp duty income and incorrectly relied on an artificial and distorted market for all their assumptions. They were economic illiterates, Government and Opposition alike. Furthermore, Brussels had been given ample warning which they completely ignored. And EU Commissioner Neelie Kroes as much as admitted this in an interview with the Dutch newspaper, *Die Telegraf*, only this March.

And when it went wrong?

They put a confiscational future tax posture into action, placing private shareholders' interests before the interests of the people. More precisely: they took money from ordinary people and put it at the disposal of the private banks. They have ineffectively imposed a huge mortgage on our children's futures. This is not Capitalism, it's economic stupidity.

Did the Government make the correct decision by bailing out the Banks?

I don't criticise the new rules for safeguarding savers' money in Banks. Libertas is proposing a joint minimum requirement to protect bank deposits. The individual saver should not have to be a financial expert with knowledge about the liquidity and viability of each and every bank.

Ordinary citizens cannot be expected to gauge the solvency of the banks in which they put their money. The public authorities must check this and pay for failures in the control system. This is only fair and every Government can require the financial institutions themselves to guarantee basic citizens deposits by means of mandatory mutual insurance. This will mean that the well-run banks will warn against the badly run ones before they run into bankruptcy. That is how to use market forces for the common good of citizens. It reflects Libertas's approach to the market economy.

We put ordinary people before shareholders' interests. We do not think it right that taxpayers, who have no rights of ownership in these banks, should be forced to pay for the inexcusable errors and casino mentality of some of these institutions.

We think that it is up to shareholders themselves to hold the company executives responsible for company management. When they witness large bonuses in dysfunctional institutions they should ask tough questions. If they do not exercise their rights of control they risk their money. That is one way the market works. You buy shares in the hope of making a profit. If you snooze you lose. Losses of that kind should never be compensated for by taxpayers. If we go around compensating any private sector loss by imposing taxes on the public we are back to a planned economy as in the Soviet Union. I have seen with my own eyes that this is a disastrous way to organise an economy.

So take note, European socialists and supporters of tax: put people first, not only in theory and rhetoric, but in practice during the current financial hurricane. And understand this: raising taxation to bail out insolvent banks will further cripple our economies and delay any prospect of dynamic recovery. It was Winston Churchill said, 'The man who thinks he can tax his way out of a recession is someone who thinks he can stand in a bucket and lift it by its handle.' On this point Churchill was right.

Where do you stand on the market economy?

Libertas understands that the market economy is the only one that works for ordinary people. Any other economic system ends up corrupted by under-the-table favouritism by politicians and bureaucrats, the doling out of Government benefits, the stifling of critical opposition and competition between economic actors, the abolition of consumer choice and the blinding of proper social oversight and confiscational levels of taxation to patch over the inefficiencies.

The whole world needs proper transparency in financial markets and joint minimum rules governing reserves before firms can enter speculative markets. If people are speculating in risk-laden ventures they should at least have some of their own money at risk. It should no longer be possible to milk taxpayers to bail out the sophisticated financial casinos that discredit the name of Capitalism and destroy the true market.

The casino economy has also resulted in extraordinarily large salaries and bonuses for the leaders of certain financial institutions. The more loans they extended, the higher their own incomes. The financial sector has simply grown out of all proportion to the real economy. The prevailing culture shifted from market to casino – and there's a hell of a difference.

The casino economy is intoxicating, but it ends up with hangovers, bad bruises and broken furniture. Worse than that, every politician who wants more of the people's money is exploiting this 'crisis' as an excuse to grab even more resources and tax our children's futures in a way that makes these politicians more powerful and subverts the real economy.

What is your alternative?

I am obviously not against banks; I like them actually. We need a healthy financial sector which provides individuals and businesses with the ability to manage savings and loans. If people come to banks with good business proposals, with the potential for real demand and real customers, yes please, that's for us. We want to stimulate innovation and encourage sensible risk-taking in the small and medium-sized business sector especially, because this is the only place from which a sustained Irish and European economic recovery is going to emerge.

This sector is the key to Ireland's and Europe's economic future and whether or not we will succeed in unlocking its potential will determine whether or not Europe can lead the world to a place worth going to. We need banks to provide easy access to loans to finance innovation. Don't forget: the laws allowing for highly leveraged investments and casino-like transactions that have brought about the present crisis have been accepted and encouraged by the major Irish political parties – both Government and Opposition – up to this point. There has been no effective voice challenging them.

8

WORKERS' RIGHTS IN THE EU

But the EU supposedly has rules protecting workers' rights? Isn't it just that they have been ignored?

Europe will have new rules. On 1 January, 2010 rules on the sale and performance of so-called economic services throughout the EU will be introduced. But these rules are unclear. And unfortunately, once again, it will be left to the European Court of Justice in Luxembourg to define their actual application. As I have already said – and it is a most important point – the people should decide the rules at EU level through their elected representatives. They should not be left to lawyers to define.

The basic Libertas principle is that every business should compete on a level playing-field.

What will be your approach to this issue?

I do not subscribe to protectionism. Throughout history protectionism has always ended in disaster – sometimes in war. I am for a free, healthy and transparent competition based on the right to private property and fair conditions where countries and businesses compete on quality, service, efficiency and price. Any artificial distortions to the market, whether they come from within Europe or outside it, need to be challenged and dealt with.

It is interesting to note that the challenge to workers' rights through the European Court has only been given token resistance by the European Socialists, yet the Court verdicts have been accepted by them. Now some of these same so-called socialists are talking about putting 'people first'. It's nauseating.

Will the coordination of economic policies affect jobs in Ireland? The Yes campaigners on Lisbon made a huge issue of a Yes vote saving jobs. The country was plastered with posters on that alone. Was it all wrong?

Unfortunately, yes. We need a new generation of politicians who are prepared to think outside the box. They will need to use all available tools to redirect risk-management for growth into more jobs and prosperity. In a strange way, this current recession could end up being the catalyst that Ireland and Europe needs. We can, if we make the right decisions, build upon fresh foundations for global economic leadership.

The USA is making some big economic mistakes at the present time. Europe has to use the unprecedented opportunities that are now available to build a competitive economic leadership. Ironically, we could then end up being the example to follow if we can find leaders prepared to lead.

Does Libertas see this time as one of opportunity?

The financial crisis demands economic coordination across the whole world and a re-organization of the international currency system. As the largest trading power in the world the EU can and should take the lead.

Countries with a surplus on their balance of payments such as Singapore, Malaysia, the oil producing countries, China, Switzerland, Taiwan and Japan – which I mention according to the relative size of their surpluses – should be encouraged to revalue their currencies or increase their demand in their domestic markets to help their own populations and encourage imports from abroad, which helps people elsewhere. If this is not done, the world will run into a much deeper recession and those countries with deficits will not be able to resist calls for the introduction of protectionist measures which could destroy the whole idea of free trade and turn the economic clock back a century.

Where will the money come from?

In the EU we also have countries with permanent surpluses on their balance of payments such as Germany, Sweden and Holland. Germany could be encouraged to increase internal spending and bring growth, particularly to their poorer regions with high unemployment. If not, the euro – the currency of 16 of the 27 EU Member States – could be at risk of collapse. The price for ten-year state bonds in Germany now varies significantly from the price for similar state bonds in Greece, Italy, Portugal, Spain and Ireland.

The only reason this is happening is that market forces are pricing in the possibility of some countries withdrawing or being withdrawn from the eurozone. Underlying factors include serious differences in the economic performances of these Member States, which need to be dealt with urgently.

And is Ireland a victim or a player?

The economic flexibility – or what is left of it – that Ireland needs would be done away with under the Lisbon Treaty. The remaining clout that we have would be severely diluted if Lisbon goes through. Our voting weight in the EU Council of Ministers would be more than halved, while that of Germany will be doubled and that of France, Britain and Italy will go up by 50%. Our concerns will be completely ignored.

As evidence of this, all you have to look at is the way our No vote was treated. Even something as powerful as the democratic voice of the Irish people is not being allowed to set these Brussels elites off their course. The Lisbon Treaty would make Ireland and many other EU Member States ignored backwaters inside the EU with no strength to defend their interests and utterly dependent on whatever crumbs Brussels might see fit to throw us.

What fiscal policies will Libertas be promoting?

Libertas will promote a close coordination of economic policies between the Member States. Countries with a budget surplus above 4% of their GNP could be asked to increase investments in the EU by, say, 10%; countries with a surplus above 2% by, say, 8%, and countries in balance by, say, 6%. EU countries with budget deficits could then afford to increase their investments as well without running into severe balance of payments problems which could cause a crisis for their participation in the euro. Such coordinated expansion would be a real expression of solidarity amongst the EU Member States.

Should Member States be allowed to opt out of the euro?

Libertas does not advocate forcing any country to remain in or enter the euro. Of course, the euro was established without the necessary means of coordinating the economies of the various countries by other than monetary means. The EU does not have common taxes and public services. It is a monetary union without being a fiscal one. This is because at its core the euro was more of a political project than an economic one. We will work to reform the euro so that the common currency facilitates the creation of jobs and prosperity – instead of just compounding the crisis.

For example, we would particularly like to make sure that start-up businesses can hire their employees without bureaucracy, regulatory burdens and red tape. I want to be very clear: Libertas is a supporter of the euro, but wants to make sure it works properly and is a help rather than a hindrance to economic recovery.

9

AGRICULTURE

Where does Libertas see the EU on farming and agri-business?

The first common policy in the EU was the Common Agricultural Policy (CAP). Its aim was to make Europe self-sufficient in food. Europe's founding fathers recognised that the bedrock of future European peace, co-operation and industrial prosperity was the home-grown supply of primary energy – food.

The CAP was very successful but ultimately, with increased technology and greatly improved farmer efficiency, over-supply of food became a problem, wine lakes and food mountains in cold storage being a result. This led to wastage and dumping of some food products on third-country markets, causing distortions and production problems in those markets.

Where do you see the problems with CAP?

The various attempts to reform the CAP have resulted in blunt bureaucratic decisions to decimate agricultural production. Farmers have been unwillingly turned into paper-pushers dependent on Brussels/Government hand-outs rather than being what most of them want to be: talented, hardworking producers whose innovation and excellence are properly rewarded.

Libertas thinks farmers should be able to make their living from farming, delivering the safe, healthy food-products that consumers are looking for at home and abroad, not being reduced to the status of paper-pushers. EU farm policies have quite unfairly turned a generation of farmers into part-time bureaucrats subservient to full-time bureaucrats in Brussels, instead of farming their crops and animals. The more recent CAP reforms of the past ten years established the Single Farm Payment (SFP) - money that is paid to farmers based on historic subsidies which have been phased out.

Has the reform of CAP helped farmers and agriculture business?

No. The so-called CAP reform has gradually impoverished farmers and reduced production dangerously. Many EU countries no longer fill their milk quotas or produce enough meat and other essential primary products. The EU expects farmers to produce food to the highest standards of quality, safety and traceability, but then expects farmers to compete in our supermarkets with unregulated imported produce. Add to this the way in which the retail food industry has concentrated into mega-supermarket chains. The net result is that EU bureaucracy has decimated farmers, and supermarket pressures and unregulated practices have driven farmgate prices below the prices that were achieved 25 years ago. Agricultural production is falling and looks like dramatically falling further on the basis of present policies.

What is Libertas's solution to the problems of the CAP?

Why not introduce an upper ceiling so that no farming business unit can receive more than €100,000 in annual subsidy from the EU? Such a ceiling will save a significant percentage of the EU budget used for agricultural subsidies. It will only hit less than 1.3 % of the farmers in the

EU and a miniscule number of farmers in Ireland. Libertas thinks farmers are better off when they can make their living from farming, delivering the healthy food produce that consumers demand here and abroad, rather than being reduced to the status of paper pushers. The EU farm policies have unfairly turned a generation of farmers into bureaucrats who spend time filling in forms instead of what they do best, which is farm.

In the case of temporary over-production, Libertas believes that more efficient systems should be used, such as Aid to Private Storage (A.P.S.) to maintain a reasonable price for farmers.

In the case of permanent over-production, we believe that impoverishing the agriculture sector is both wasteful and dangerous. Surplus land and capacity should be used for industrial applications and for the production of green energy.

This would tie into the Libertas approach to alternative energy.

New technologies for turning grass products into plastics are very exciting. Energy crops from our cereal farmers will help Europe to become less dependent on energy imports. Farmers will respond to the positive solutions and leadership that Libertas will provide.

What are your views on the subject of farm produce and farm incomes?

It makes sense for the Union as one to facilitate one market for healthy food products. We'll advocate commonsense quality-assurance schemes and food-safety regulations. We'll insist that food imports comply with EU standards without exception. While recognising that organic food production is for niche markets, we will encourage organic and artisan food production.

At the same time, our commitment to a policy of slashing bureaucracy will ease the stress and unnecessary time wasted for farmers, giving them the freedom to farm. At times of temporarily difficult market conditions – such as the milk sector at present – Libertas will press for EU support systems to be activated quickly and efficiently. We champion the true value of farmers as custodians of our countryside and their vital contribution to preserving our natural heritage and environment. Libertas will ensure that future EU Environmental Schemes such as REPS will receive proper resources to encourage greater farmer participation.

10

THE BRUSSELS LOBBY SYSTEM

Who pays for all the things the EU does?

There are at least 15,000 professional lobbyists – and probably more – now *working* Brussels with the aim of influencing EU laws, so obtaining some form of EU subsidy for their clients. This puts Brussels on a par or ahead of Washington when it comes to lobbyists living off the system.

But the EU does not have its own budget to pay for this. In reality every single cent spent comes from the taxpayers in the Member States. It is you and I who finance the EU every time we buy a product in a shop. A part of the nationally collected VAT – 1 % of the price of all products - goes to Brussels. Most customs and import duties also go to finance the EU. For instance, if you buy a bike from Japan you will pay 15% of the price to Brussels.

Another source of EU revenue is that all fines paid by companies for breaches of EU regulations go to Brussels. This system seems to target large companies with deep pockets. One could not be blamed for thinking that it looks like a shakedown and revenue-raising exercise for Brussels rather than a championing of consumer interests. Member States also pay a direct contribution based on the size of their GNP. In these ways part of the taxes you pay your Government are put at the disposal of the bureaucrats in Brussels.

What does business think of all these Brussels regulations?

Early this year I was told by a senior American corporate lawyer that because of the ease of introducing business regulation in Brussels out of sight of the media or public, he knew of cases where US companies lobbied for particular EU regulations and then took cases against their competitors in the US alleging breaches of EU rules.

These American companies found EU law easier to manipulate than US law back in America. I was surprised to see the *Financial Times* running a story last year that effectively praised Brussels for being the world's 'leader' in setting standards and regulations. As if more regulation and more restrictive so-called standards are in the best interests of the public!

I have often seen at first hand in business how established systems and regulations are abused to protect products and companies from competitors offering better services at lower prices. Where such standards can be introduced by new EU rules, one needs to look warily at who is lobbying for them, who is drafting them, and how they end up on our statute books. Brussels has become one of the best places in the world to smuggle in unsuitable laws, standards and inappropriate specifications for goods and services. The system there is wide open to corruption to the detriment of the public interest. The fact that very few people know about it makes it even more vulnerable to abuse.

And how has Ireland done over the years regarding EU finances?

In Ireland, since we joined the then EEC in 1973, we received more Brussels money each year than we paid in contributions. We have been bigger EU beneficiaries than contributors. In the next couple of years, however, we should start to pay more money to Brussels than we receive from the EU budget. I think that is fair enough as we have to do our fair share of the lifting.

Despite the recession, when the time comes Ireland should be able to afford to contribute more into the pot than the poorest Member States. Libertas MEPs will obviously vote in favour of focusing EU subsidies on the poorest citizens and regions of the poorest Member States.

Are you against EU subsidies as such?

Of course not, but only when they are appropriate. We need to stop the flow of subsidies to large rich companies who tend to be better at lobbying for them in Brussels because they can spend more money in hiring expensive lobbyists. Their smaller competitors cannot afford to spend such sums in rooting for protectionist subsidies. Many EU subsidies would never have been implemented if they had to be agreed by taxpayers in the Member States.

Where do you see change in the EU subsidy regime coming from?

Our economy will grow from good framework conditions that promote innovation. It will not flourish on the basis of a system of subsidies fostered by an artificial and ever-expanding lobby industry. Why should I work to increase the number of Irish lobbyists in Brussels who produce nothing of real value.

I always think that people's money is better left in their own pockets than in the pockets of the Brussels bureaucrats and lobbyists. Am I wrong to say that when subsidies are coming from EU taxpayers, accountability and transparency should be the priority? We need to know where the call for a subsidy originated, who initiated it, who was involved in deciding on the subsidy, what relation they have to the beneficiaries, how long is the subsidy needed for and why, and what alternative to it has been considered. We need to enquire whether these alternatives might not be better than providing a subsidy in the first place. We need to ask whether providing the subsidy is in the best interest of consumers and the general public or just those benefiting from the subsidy. We need to ask who is representing or lobbying for the subsidy and have they publicly registered their interests as lobbyists? All this is very important.

What is your thinking on EU taxation?

Pretty straightforward and simple – taxes should be low and regularly justified to those whose money the Government is taking. The EU today collects taxes from citizens, companies and Member States of up to 1.27% of the total EU annual gross product. That adds up to a lot of money. Serious consideration needs to be given to capping the level of EU tax, stealth tax or otherwise. We should seek to ensure that the EU is not paying for anything anywhere that it would not be allowed to do under the laws of any of its Member States.

Would the Lisbon Treaty make any difference to how the EU is funded?

The various kinds of EU revenue I have mentioned are known in Brussels jargon as the EU's 'own resources'. Article 311 of the new EU Treaty as amended by Lisbon would add to them significantly by allowing the EU Governments to impose any tax to raise new revenue for the EU – income tax, sales tax, wealth tax or whatever – without any need for further treaties or referendums, so long as they agreed that unanimously among themselves.

The EU Prime Ministers would have every incentive to agree to that, in my view, for it would endow the EU centrally, where the Prime Ministers call the shots, with the resources to finance the many new policies that Lisbon envisages. If the Prime Ministers and Governments want a system of direct EU taxes, I cannot see any National Parliament standing in the way.

Where has the EU got it wrong regarding money?

In my opinion the whole approach to the culture of taxation in the EU is wrongheaded. There is an absolute sense of entitlement among beneficiaries of the various EU programmes and a quite immoral disregard for the people whose money is being taken from them and spent by Brussels – and that is all of us. Right now, if you don't like the way Brussels is spending your money there is virtually nothing you can do about it. And remember the EU is actually facilitating the lifting and expenditure of your money in ways that are not reflected in the official EU Budget because the true cost of many EU policies end up being incurred at Member State level and it can run into billions. In fact, it is difficult to get an accurate figure of total EU-related spending because it is so obscure.

Is there much EU extravagance? Could the EU be more frugal?

There should be much more care taken of taxpayers' money by MEPs. For example, parliamentarians voted to renovate sports facilities with the costs standing at a staggering €9.2 million. All for a new sauna and swimming pool for themselves. This is just wrong during the onset of mass layoffs across Europe, with families being put on the breadline. This kind of extravagance is utterly removed from reality and quite disgusting. What makes it really gut-wrenching is that the Parliamentarians are not doing this with their own money but with your money. They presume nobody is watching because until Libertas came along very few people were.

Even more importantly, it is absolutely and categorically the intention of Brussels to introduce a harmonised tax base and eventually a harmonised tax rate that will prevail all over Europe. The Irish Government can shout all they like that this is not the case, but everyone in Brussels knows full well that it is.

I am as sure as it is possible to be that the only reason the French did not push through measures to harmonise the tax base during their EU presidency was because we voted No to the Lisbon Treaty in Ireland last year. Christine Lagarde, the French Finance Minister, stated at a conference in the run-up to the Irish referendum that tax harmonisation across the EU would be a priority for the French presidency. The wishful-thinkers in our own Government and Opposition and the leadership of IBEC still went around calling for a Yes vote to Lisbon last year when there is ample evidence of the EU's intention – and particularly the intention of some in Germany, France and Britain – to move on harmonising taxes in the EU at the first opportunity.

There was further evidence when German Chancellor Merkel's party spokesman on finance, Otto Bernhardt, said in March that a fund existed to assist eurozone countries if needs be, but that, 'We will not tolerate there being low-tax countries like Ireland for example. We will insist on a minimum corporation tax rate.'

How do different countries fare regarding money in the EU?

When Ireland, the UK and Denmark joined the then

EEC in 1973 we only paid 20% of our calculated contribution in the first year, 40 % in the second, 60 % in the third, 80% in the fourth and the full amount only after five years.

Denmark and the UK were rich countries, Ireland a poor country, but we all got these initial rebates. Now the EU is demanding that the poorest countries coming from Communist poverty should pay 100% from their first year of membership. This is simply not fair, in my view. This is again Brussels acting as the Sheriff of Nottingham rather than Robin Hood. Libertas members in the European Parliament will propose a rebate for the poorest countries which should last until they have reached a certain level of economic development. We will also oppose any discrimination against the new Member States in the distribution of agricultural subsidies.

How should this rebate be estimated?

We will calculate the amounts to be paid to Poland, Romania and the other new Member States without discrimination and then offer these amounts for their own development. These are much poorer countries. They belong to a category to which Ireland belonged when it first joined the EU: that of the new and poor Member States. Lifting these economies and consumer markets is clearly in the interest of producers in France, Germany, the UK, Spain, Italy, Ireland and all Member States.

Let us talk about research and energy.

Libertas has been working on a sustainable energy policy since well before last year's Irish referendum. I see four primary drivers that make energy policy a crucial component of any future Government programme in Europe. First, the need for access by the consumer industry to an affordable, reliable and uninterrupted energy supply. Second, security of supply. Europe cannot be exposed to overdependence on any single source of supply or technology. We need to spread the risks. Third, environmental considerations, in particular the effects on manmade global warming. These need to be factored into and shape Europe's future energy plans. Fourth, real as opposed to perceived costs of dependence on certain areas for energy supply.

For example, over-dependence on imported oil is not only bad for the environment but it has a real cost in terms of global security. It can have a distorting effect on democratic and accountable governance in countries that earn easy money by pumping oil without having to depend on a domestic tax base and without having to look for popular support for democratic policies. All of these factors lead to instability, not just in prices and reliability of supply, but in international security, with implications for the global balance of power.

Libertas has proposed a radical approach to unlocking innovation in the pursuit of discovering and developing new cost-competitive energy alternatives. We have proposed launching a Europe-wide competition for this end and have given details on our web-site.

How do you see the geo-politics of energy?

Energy policy is an area of innovation where I want to see Europe take a world leadership position. I want to see the energy policy of the mid to late 21st century world based on technology, innovation and industry leadership that originate in the European Union.

The past two years experience of interruptions of Russian gas supplies as part of a game of 'real politik' between Russia and Western Europe is something that is really unacceptable. Russia is home to some of the world's finest remaining gas reserves. Their proven and unproven size far exceed those of Norway, the UK and anywhere else in Europe. Europe needs to come to a sensible understanding with our Russian friends whereby they understand that we are good customers of theirs, but that we have other credible options - and we need to make sure we have them – and that they cannot dictate to us which European countries their supply lines will traverse and which ones they will avoid. The current way in which Russia has been carving Poland and other countries out of the gas supply-line map does not bode well for the future.

In dealing with overseas energy suppliers, including Russia, we must look carefully at the influences that are shaping European energy policy. The fact that the former socialist Chancellor of Germany, Gerhard Schröder, would have been instrumental in influencing EU policy, particularly in the area of gas, and then ends up as Vice-Chairman of Gazprom, which is Europe's largest gas supplier and is effectively controlled from the Kremlin, has to give rise to serious concern. Relationships with the EU's major oil suppliers need to be looked at with a friendly yet cautious eye. The vulnerability to corruption and graft of the EU system that makes most of our laws is truly alarming. It would be surprising if it was not being exploited by interests that do not have Europe's energy interests at heart. For now, all we can do is hope this isn't happening.

Europe must have a strong, agreed energy policy. If it has not, the European project puts itself at enormous risk of failure. Energy is one of the important areas where the Union offers the only credible path and tools to provide a long-term solution.

11

EU MIGRATION AND OTHER ISSUES

Is the easy movement of people satisfactory in today's Europe?

I do not think so. The original intention was that the Union would facilitate the right of people to move across borders to seek employment, get married and so on. However, after all these years the Union does not function well or fairly in this respect and yet at the same time it has utterly failed to implement a fair and effective strategy to tackle illegal immigration. This has enabled organized crime to exploit the system and traffic illegal immigrants for exploitation, drugs, arms, and other unlawful or immoral activities.

We need a thorough overhaul of the present system to facilitate the ease of movement of European citizens and at the same time have a fair, equitable and moral immigration policy. We absolutely need to close down the underground systems that are playing havoc with our border controls and personnel, especially in those Member States where most immigrants first enter the EU. There are some real horror stories in this area which we do not have the time and space to go into now. There is a lot of dirty money sloshing around the EU borders as regards illegal trafficking and the like which is wearing away the system at its edges.

Side by side with that there is some nightmarish red-tape to be faced by people who want to work or study in other Member States. Students with EU scholarships often receive grants too late to facilitate ease of movement. We need to minimise the bureaucracy and cost for students and workers from one Member State who just want to spend a year or two gaining experience, know-how and new friends in other Member States. The types of lifelong relationships and friendships that can flourish through this kind of interaction are essential if we want to create a real sense of what it means to be European.

What would you do about it?

Libertas will work towards establishing one joint 'blue card' for all Member State citizens, allowing them to settle in another country for up to two years without bureaucracy. EU citizens would simply apply for the card on the Internet, with appropriate identity verification and controls, and would obtain the right to work or study in another Member State on the strict proviso that the student or worker would be independent and would not seek economic help from the host Member State. So, no dole, no rent subsidy, no hand-outs – work study, explore, volunteer, but do not expect support from other countries' taxpayers. Health and other social benefits should remain a matter for your Member State of origin. Such an approach would save a lot of money, time and energy and would really encourage young people to work and study across the Union.

If a person needs access to use the local schools or other state-financed facilities, they may apply for domicile in their new country on the same basis as today. This 'blue card' system would not encourage social tourism. The costs of social and health insurance must be paid for by the home country or a person's employer. The EU budget could eventually finance a part of the necessary cost of this system for the poorest Member States.

What is your position on global warming?

Libertas wants the EU to be active in the fight against man-made global warming. As I said in an earlier interview, we see the development of a green economy as being a means for major economic growth in the new energy sector. The challenge of man-made global warming is a good example of an issue which needs to be dealt with at the transnational EU level.

Some years ago my wife Delia and I had the honour of hosting former US Vice-President Al Gore at our home in Tuam. I share some of his ideas on how to tackle man-made global warming. In my view our current approach to the environment does a disservice to future generations. We have to change this while always remembering that we must help those living in the present as well as making the necessary investment for the future.

Moving on to the subject of education, what should the EU be focusing on to ensure quality education for future generations?

Education is one of those areas where Member States should continue to have responsibility for their own citizens. However, as I said earlier, we absolutely should make a serious investment at the EU level to establish higher education 'centres of excellence' for Third-Level, so that Europe has institutions that can excel and compete with the likes of Harvard and MIT. These centres of excellence could be new establishments or - and this would be my personal preference - we could focus on some existing institutions and seek to raise their standards, investments and the range of intellectual and scientific choices available. I like to think of this as an idea for new 'Renaissance Universities' in the EU.

I raise this idea because we want to have a competitive economy in Europe 20 years from now. To help achieve this we must possess the best universities and research facilities in the world. We cannot leave this to the Brussels bureaucracy. I very much doubt their abilities and judgment in this area. There is a question of democratic will here: can we persuade the people of Europe to understand just how badly we need these 'centres of excellence'? The people need to get behind a vision of radically improved education across the EU so as to empower decision-makers to make this a European policy priority and allocate the necessary resources.

12

CITIZENSHIP

Where does Libertas stand on the idea of EU citizenship as opposed to national?

The Lisbon Constitution/Treaty creates an 'additional' and separate citizenship of the new Union which it would legally establish. There are a couple of important points here. It's important to note – and I suspect many of our politicians and media people have entirely missed this – that the Lisbon Treaty dissolves the European Community which has existed since the 1957 Founding Treaty of Rome and which Ireland joined in 1973. In its place it creates a new legal entity, the Union, which for the first time would be constitutionally separate from and superior to its 27 Member States. The new Union – via the Lisbon Treaty (which again is really a Constitution) would make us all citizens of the European Union 'in addition to', not 'complementary to' (and there's a big difference) our National citizenship.

Let me put this another way. Let's say you are a French citizen and you also have American citizenship. Your American citizenship would be in addition to your French citizenship and your French citizenship would be in addition to your American one. They are not complementary to each other, insofar as that if you were in America, as an American citizen you would be entirely subject to American laws; and in front of an American judge, the fact that you had an additional French citizenship would not make a blind bit of difference to that judge, nor should it. Likewise if you were in front of a French judge under French law, the fact that you had an additional American passport wouldn't make a blind bit of difference to that judge, nor should it. What is the reason for this? The reason is that all French citizens are equal before the laws of France, as all American citizens are equal before the laws of the USA.

Under the Lisbon Treaty, because we will become additionally European citizens, all 500 million Europeans will be equal before the laws of Europe, which are superior to the laws of the Member States, because the Lisbon Treaty in its Declaration on Primacy makes clear that this is the case. 'The laws of the Union shall have primacy over the laws of the Member States.' This is game, set and match to the laws of the Union. Anybody who thinks that Member State law would be allowed to overrule or contradict Union law is delusional.

Why?

Because even if the Member States were under the false impression that their laws would remain supreme for their citizens, they are wrong on a number of fronts, including this important point that their citizens are no longer just their citizens – they now become the citizens of a separate additional entity, the Union, whose laws are made supreme by the Lisbon Treaty/Constitution. Politicians everywhere have buried their heads in the sand on this point because if they were to admit what is actually happening they would have to admit that they have made us legal subjects and citizens of an entity whose Constitution and structures are truly anti-democratic. We are being made citizens of a Union with an unelected and unaccountable President and an unelected and unaccountable structure that initiates our laws. This truly is post-democracy and it's very bloody dangerous.

If we are going to have this European citizenship – and Libertas agrees with this – it can only happen if the citizens of Europe can hold the leaders of Europe democratically accountable. Any such arrangement must be clear that it respects Europe's cultural diversity and the traditions and wishes of the individual Member States. This European citizenship cannot be used as a back door by activist judges in the European Court to create new citizens' rights and entitlements in Member States where those rights and entitlements are in contradiction to the laws of those states.

So let me speak very clearly here. No declaration by the EU Prime Ministers to help out Brian Cowen and no political promise that may be tagged on to the Lisbon Treaty/Constitution will change a single thing as outlined above. This is one of the many reasons why the Lisbon Treaty has to be binned and we have to start from scratch with a new basic Treaty of no more than 25 pages or so.

This is truly shocking. Do you have anything to add on this point?

This is an obviously massive constitutional change, yet it is something which most people – and I would say almost everyone on the Yes side in Ireland – have absolutely no idea about because decent people, who are democrats, would never agree to such a thing if they knew about it, and I include most of Ireland's politicians in that. I would guess that the number of citizens in all the 27 Member States who are aware of these huge constitutional changes being made by Lisbon number no more than a few thousand out of nearly 500 million. This is a democratic outrage and it is information that, I believe, has been hidden deliberately from the people of Europe. I very much hope this will encourage Attorney-Generals and judges to scramble through their law books to find out. If they want a copy of the Lisbon Treaty and how it would amend the existing European Treaties we will happily send them one, and I don't mean that to be rude or disrespectful in any way. Libertas will also ensure that there is a full text of the Treaty available on our website, www.libertas.eu.

Will we lose our foreign policy under the Lisbon Treaty?

Of course we do. I mean how can we keep it? In fact, I don't even have a fundamental problem with the idea of a common EU foreign policy if the EU leadership and decision-making structures are democratically accountable. Indeed, there are many good reasons why it makes sense to have a common foreign security and defence policy. No single European Member State can pack a credible punch in the world today, and Europe has become over-reliant on the concept of soft power. Soft power is clearly the best and most palpable to exercise, but it is never credible unless your counterparts understand that you also possess credible hard power. Otherwise you can never be taken seriously by those who may seek to do Europe harm.

What we have with the Lisbon Treaty is the outline structure for a common European foreign policy. A de facto Ministry of Foreign Affairs and EU military structures are being built for 27 Member States and probably 30 or more in the future. Making such a policy fit for Germany, the UK, Romania, Latvia, Finland, Ireland, Greece etc. is frankly going to be, let us say, difficult. However, that is not to say it cannot be done but it certainly won't work unless the people of Europe are wholeheartedly behind it.

Is an EU foreign policy already taking place?

You could say it is. Even now Brussels and Member States' governments are not even waiting for the adoption of the already rejected Lisbon Treaty – they are pressing on with the institutional arrangements, regardless of the democratic voice. There is a plan to establish EU embassies across the globe and a separate EU diplomatic service – to make it clear to other countries that the EU is like a 'State'. The EU will have its own so-called 'legal personality' if the Lisbon Treaty/Constitution is ratified. This means that the EU will negotiate with other States in the world and sign international Treaties with them just as a Member State does.

If things go on like this Ireland and the other Member States will slowly disappear as separate and distinct factors from the international diplomatic scene. If the Lisbon Treaty is ratified that could happen very quickly. We might be left with our own United Nations membership – it will be interesting to see how they handle that. Member States' Departments of Foreign Affairs will have less and less to do over the years. Their senior civil servants will be pensioned off or moved to grander portfolios within the EU Foreign Ministry in Brussels. I would not be at all surprised if these new jobs didn't come with a second pension also!

Where would the policy of a post-Lisbon EU be shaped, challenged, altered?

Much of it would be done in Luxembourg by the judges of the EU Court. This means even more power passing to the flawed process of law-making that we talked about earlier. It will raise huge issues of redefinition so far as human rights are concerned. The activist EU Court in Luxembourg will develop joint EU rights for EU citizens on their own. They have done this in the past, even before they were ever given the full right to do so.

The Lisbon Treaty effectively gives them this right by making the EU Charter of Fundamental Rights legally binding for the first time. We will soon see the fundamental rights of EU citizens being regulated on the EU level independently of and superior to the human rights provisions of Member State Constitutions.

There may well be some EU Court verdicts we will like and some we won't like. We simply don't know in advance. There might be much tighter control on freedom of expression for civil servants, for example. Or less stringent controls regarding the use of hard drugs, or whatever. Human rights issues can crop up in a multitude of contexts. Under the Lisbon Treaty, all sorts of human rights matters for 500 million EU citizens would be decided by the EU Court of Justice in Luxembourg, just as they do today at the Court of Human Rights in Strasbourg.

For Libertas it is still important to respect the National Constitutions of our Member States in such politically sensitive areas as human rights. Given the existing democratic deficit in Brussels, I am not prepared to have Member State Constitutions subjugated to the EU Court on these matters – at least not yet. I value the integrity of the Member States and the democratic character of their Constitutions above the Lisbon Treaty formula for giving power over human rights to Brussels.

The Lisbon Treaty/Constitution puts the anti-democratic institutions in Brussels above everything, and unless and until they are democratised, such a development should not be acceptable to any European. That is why we need a clear upfront and honest 25-page

Treaty/Constitution in place of the Lisbon Treaty/
Constitution.

13

POLICING AND CRIME

Let's move on to the issue of policing within an EU-wide context. What are your thoughts on this issue?

I have some degree of insight into European police cooperation. At one point I even made an address to the European Parliament's Joint Police Working Group. I have also hired the former deputy leader of Europol, Kevin O'Connell, to work with Libertas and since doing that Kevin has offered to be a candidate for the European elections in the UK; he really is a top-notch individual.

In summary, our position begins with money. A lot of money is wasted on a badly run European police headquarters in The Hague. The necessary police cooperation across the EU can be organized both more cheaply and better. Law enforcement cooperation can be handled in a vastly more effective way than today. If we get the electoral mandate we are looking for, we will send Kevin O'Connell to the special committee in the European Parliament that deals with joint police cooperation. They won't pull the wool over Kevin's eyes – he knows better.

Cooperation in law enforcement and networking by the bodies responsible is essential in the European Union. It is there already but it does not meet Libertas's standards. Such cross-national cooperation needs to be properly scrutinised by the National Parliaments and the European Parliament. It is vital and necessary that Member States cooperate in the exchange of intelligence about terrorism, people trafficking, cross-national crime and things like that and there is a need for vast improvement in this area.

What about covert security and terrorist surveillance?

The EU Secret Services, under their various names, need to be scrutinised to prevent misuse and abuse of their extensive powers, especially when those powers are being targeted at fellow-European citizens and law-abiding organisations. Otherwise people will lose confidence and the credibility of these essential services will be undermined. Confidence in the integrity of Europe's security services is an absolute necessity if we want to defend our open societies and civilization.

Libertas will be a determined defender and committed friend of law enforcement and security for the protection of Europe's interests and the interests of the privacy of citizens, the freedom of individuals and families throughout the EU. We will do whatever we can to ensure that law enforcement and security services are adequately resourced with funding and personnel so as to be able to do their jobs effectively.

When you talk of secret services being scrutinized, does it really happen? Are there not some people in reality who are above the law?

Well, take for example Europol civil servants who at present under the EU Treaties have immunity from prosecution if they commit a crime themselves. This is clearly wrong. Libertas will advocate removing such immunity and putting these organisations under scrutiny by a special committee in the European Parliament. This committee should be able to receive and handle confidential law enforcement information. This committee, or more likely a separate committee, could also cover the new intelligence cooperation within the Union. We will also advocate removing immunity from prosecution in the European Parliament. It is outrageous that some MEPs can hide behind the immunity from prosecution that is currently given to them.

For example, take Minister Dick Roche's friend, Daniel Cohn-Bendit MEP. Not so long ago the German Public Prosecutor requested the European Parliament to lift his immunity from prosecution. This was to allow him to be questioned about allegedly providing accommodation in his home for a wanted terrorist suspect whom the police sought for questioning over his role in a murder and kidnapping case.

The European Parliament refused to lift Cohn-Bendit's immunity to allow him to be interrogated about this matter. Cohn-Bendit was the prominent MEP who called in the European Parliament for me to be investigated as a possible CIA agent! The implication was that I was someone who was trying to undermine Europe. The Irish Government and various people in the media took up this piece of dirt and tried to use it against Libertas. They were not in the least inclined to defend my integrity against that of Danny Cohn-Bendit.

How did we arrive at this system of immunity from prosecution when in your eyes it is so defective?

The basic problem is that rules are made in secret working-groups in Brussels. We have talked about this already in general terms, but it becomes an even more urgent matter when it concerns public and personal safety, the vetting of EU personnel and the like. The trouble is that we have no idea of what goes on in these secret working-groups and so we are unable to influence them or check on what they are doing and why. There is zero transparency.

In our view it is the National Parliaments and the

European Parliament that must decide what efforts need to be employed against real terrorist threats. Only in that way can we mobilise the support of ordinary citizens. If institutions have a democratic mandate, people will be more likely to respect them and back them, which in turn will help ensure that organised criminals, along with the likes of Al Qaeda terrorist cells, can be more easily infilitrated and put out of business.

Where does Libertas stand on Civil Liberties?

Civil liberties and the fight against terrorism are also a vital issues for the Union. It is essential that we fight terrorism with every resource at our disposal but we must never forget our civic freedoms and civil liberties because these are the vital essence of what we are seeking to defend. Ireland has helped to shape the EU, making our own national contribution as a society where we can feel free to express our views and have the right to meet and organise freely. We must get the balance right.

Benjamin Franklin, one of America's founding fathers, said once, 'Those who give up a little freedom to attain a little security deserve neither and will surely lose both.' Those words are as true for Europe today as they were for the founders of America back in the late 1700s.

14

FOREIGN RELATIONS

Are you for or against the accession of Turkey to the EU?

The issue of Turkey is a lightning rod and there are strong feelings on the subject across Europe. Put simply, Turkish accession would require unanimity amongst all the existing Member States and on such a pivotal question referendums may be the only way to go.

For the foreseeable future Libertas MEPs will have a free vote of conscience on this issue. Personally, I have real reservations. However, the question needs to be asked, 'What does Turkey do and where does it go if not into Europe?' We need to help Turkey find the right answer.

What about the notion of expulsion from the EU? Surely there are scare tactics being applied to the probable next referendum, based on the idea that we may be put out? Isn't all the emphasis on staying at the heart of Europe?

This is a vital issue, particularly in view of the widespread presentation of Ireland as being in danger of some kind of expulsion from the EU.

Just as we cannot bring in a new Member State without unanimity, so it is the case that we cannot remove a Member State without the same unanimity. The truth of the matter is simply this: so long as Ireland or any other

Member State wishes to remain in the EU it has an imprescriptible right so to remain.

There is no mechanism for the removal of any Member State from the Union. It cannot be done. This is especially so over an issue such as the ratification or rejection of the Lisbon Treaty/Constitution.

To quote Irish Commissioner Charlie McCreevy's famous interview in *Hot Press* magazine last December, '*There is no provision in the existing treaties to isolate anybody. There is no provision to throw out anybody, unless unanimously all the existing members of the club agreed to throw you out. And I doubt, now or in the future, any Irish government is going to unanimously agree to throw themselves out.*'

Can we deal with defence and respect for neutrality?

I've served as a member of the Irish Reserve Defence Forces and therefore have a smattering of practical experience of being a part-time foot soldier. The 27 Member States have chosen different approaches to the matter of defence. Most Member States are also members of NATO along with the US and Canada. Others are neutral. We must obviously respect the choice of each individual Member State.

The Irish government takes a *laissez-faire* approach to neutrality. For example, when they take part in close military cooperation in the EU, Ireland does this even in areas where the NATO member Denmark abstains from participation.

Do you think Ireland is confused over the issue of neutrality?

Ireland has been confused about neutrality for decades. The country, no matter who is leading it, simply does not understand the realities of modern terrorism and conflict. I happen to believe that neutrality is not consistent with membership of a European Union that is fully democratic, which people wholeheartedly support and with which they freely identify. I see it like this: you are part of a family, sharing at the table, and sharing all the benefits. When someone tries to kick the door down at night-time you refuse to come to the family's help. You do not say, 'Sorry, I'm neutral.' Such a position is patently immoral. You are either part of a family with all of the benefits and responsibilities of that family, or you are not. If we expect all the good things of membership of a worthwhile Union, you have also to share in the difficulties, and these can go as far as the defence of territory and resistance to attack. One hopes that such threats belong to the past, but history teaches us differently.

The theory and practice of military and security defence are hampered by a doctrinaire hang-up about neutrality. Throughout history, Ireland has provided the world with some of its greatest soldiers. Irish soldiers today proudly continue that great tradition and they are often not sufficiently appreciated for what they do and for the resource they provide in making a serious contribution to Ireland's international interests and the cause of peace both in Europe and around the world.

Why do you refer to the upcoming European elections as being in part a proxy vote on the Lisbon Treaty? You also refer to it as a referendum on Ireland's national political elites?

A proper and healthy democracy means, in my view, that no one is above the Irish people in Ireland, or above the German people in Germany or the French people in France. Similarly, there should be no one above the citizens of Europe having the right to govern themselves without our granting them that right through the ballot box.

Therefore, because of the effects of the Lisbon Treaty on such fundamental matters, it absolutely should be put to a referendum in all of the other Member States before anyone even asks for a second referendum in Ireland.

It is, to me, an absolute disgrace and truly unintelligent that we have a Government that has not only accepted, but has even conspired, to hold a referendum twice on exactly the same text. They have done this while still allowing the silencing of the French and Dutch No-votes to the EU Constitution to stand. That Constitution is now embodied in the Lisbon Treaty. It is shameful that none of the leaders of Europe have had the moral decency to ask their own people to vote on this historic issue.

Irish Ministers and senior civil servants have urged the other Member States to ratify the Treaty after the sovereign citizens of Ireland rejected it – as did the French and Dutch before them. These Ministers and civil servants deliberately sought to isolate Ireland diplomatically on the issue of the Lisbon Treaty. In former times there were simple words for this type of action by these types of people. The words are treachery and betrayal. Their actions are an absolute disgrace to the name of Ireland and the fundamentals of democracy.

The Irish Government and French President, Nicolas Sarkozy, want us to feel ashamed for having rejected a Treaty which would have been rejected in most other Member States as well, as Sarkozy himself has said.

In December 2008, the 27 European Prime Ministers held a summit in Brussels. They decided that there would not be one single amendment to the Treaty we voted against.

What about the details of what the Lisbon re-run will ask?

The legal text of Lisbon will be identical. It cannot be changed. The Amendment we are being asked to insert into the Irish Constitution to enable the State to ratify it, to be a member of the new European Union which Lisbon would establish, and to give the 'laws, acts and measures' of this new Union superiority over the Irish Constitution and laws, must be identical also. The referendum will be accompanied by some political window-dressing. There will be various 'clarifications and interpretative agreements' that will not change a comma of the Lisbon Treaty.

If the misfortune should happen that Lisbon would come into force, it would thereafter be interpreted by the EU Court of Justice, and not on the basis of these political declarations and clarifications. In effect the EU Constitution which the French and Dutch peoples rejected in 2005 will be presented to Irish voters in a separate envelope. This was the image that former French President V. Giscard d'Estaing used when he compared the two documents.

This is why one of the motivations for voters across the EU is to use the European elections in June 2009 to vote against the political elite that seeks to foist this anti-democratic Lisbon Constitution upon them. The economic crisis will also be central to those elections – and on that issue European political leaders have zero credibility. They need to be held to account for this as well.

15

THE TRUTH BEHIND THE INNUENDOS

Let's discuss Libertas's spending during the referendum campaign? A figure of €1.3 million is being speculated upon.

It was in the region of €800,000. We didn't pay the full list price for anything. Like any business, we negotiated. When you see the Government throwing out these exaggerated figures, based upon their estimates of costs, is it any wonder the economy is in so much trouble?

The question the people on the Yes side want an answer to is: *how* **did Libertas fund its referendum campaign?**

The campaign was financed by fundraising and initially a €200,000 loan facility that I put in place. We started fundraising at the start of 2008 when I invited a few people over to my house to discuss starting a campaign. I know our Opposition is constantly asking, 'Who funded Libertas?' It would be entirely inappropriate to divulge a list of contributors as there could be some repercussions for these supporters by a vindictive Irish political cartel. If we are to give the names of our donors in the future, everyone would have to do it. Fair is fair. And still, the Yes side goes unquestioned about where it got the millions of euro to fund its campaigns. This is truly laughable.

Are you able to name any prominent supporters?

Ulick McEvaddy came out very early as a prominent supporter. Within days the Fine Gael Party as well as certain media outlets began to attack him. Fine Gael even accused him of being some kind of front for the CIA or Pentagon interests. Ulick was given a very hard time, but he's as tough as nails and he was able to take it and keep on smiling.

The attack on Ulick led others to ask me to protect their identities. They were concerned that they would be similarly targeted. I believe there was subtle – and not so subtle – intimidation in this. It was aimed at our donor base. It was also aimed at potential donors. It did not stop a very large number of people from helping, but it may have lessened some bigger potential personal commitments to Libertas.

Do you feel there is a personalised animus against you?

That is there, but I think I can deal with it. There is also a demonising of Libertas which we, who run it, find a bit more difficult because it involves continual misrepresentation of what we stand for, combined with aspersions on the integrity of what we do.

When we hosted the dinner for President Klaus of the Czech Republic, we had to furnish the Government with a list of attendees. This was for security reasons. Somehow, someone somewhere leaked the guest list to *The Irish Times*. They published it.

Do you know where they got it?

Interestingly, the guest list we gave to the government had one incorrect name on it. Sometimes these people are predictable: the list with the incorrect name was the one that made it into *The Irish Times*.

The point is that President Klaus attended two dinner functions while on his State visit to Ireland. One of these was the privately-funded Libertas dinner and one was funded by taxpayers. *The Irish Times* published a full list of those attending the private function but didn't publish the list of those wining and dining at the taxpayers' expense.

Did you resent this?

It was an elegant form of what passes in other papers for gutter-press journalism, but is represented by *The Irish Times* as a bit of 'public service'. During the present campaign for the expected re-run of the Lisbon Treaty referendum, which the paper lost the last time, it is doing all in its power to discredit myself and my organisation.

Is there an agenda here?

What is there is self-evident. Surely, by now, everybody understands that the main Yes campaigner is not the Government but Editor Geraldine Kennedy and her team at *The Irish Times*? They lost any credibility on the subject long before last year's vote was held and they've only got worse since then. At a press conference in Vilnius, a Lithuanian journalist told me that the Soviets in the old days would never have made their political agenda so obvious in their media. It is shameful because *The Irish Times*, on so many other issues, is a decent newspaper with decent people working there.

Would you want your name to be on a dinner list and published in *The Irish Times*? When that happened, during the Czech President's visit at the end of last year, it was simply a contemptible piece of journalism, unworthy of a good newspaper.

What is difficult on the personal side?

There are two components. The first is that they keep referring to me as a multi-millionaire. This presentation of Declan Ganley gives potential donors the impression that

I have limitless amounts of money to throw at the campaigns I support. That is clearly daft, but it is also malicious.

It would be entirely self-defeating as well as being, in many cases, illegal for me to be the primary ongoing source of funds for Libertas. And for Libertas not to have a broad donor base, which is absolutely essential for any political party or movement, would mean we would not be viable. We have to look to the intermediate term. Our mission, as a party and as an organisation, has to work in the future. We absolutely need small donors – eventually many hundreds of thousands of them – to meet this challenge. It is always important that no political party or movement becomes overly dependent on a handful of large donors – and even worse if they become dependent on taxpayer resourced funding, which would detach them from any kind of popular legitimacy and would tend to result in them trying to stifle new competitors by closing off avenues to funding.

And you must have money coming in from outside?

As I said, for this we must have donors, small and not so small, which thankfully we have. Smaller donors are actually even more important because they broaden the base of committed supporters. Our political opponents convey the impression that money is no obstacle to Libertas. This is a tactic designed to put off potential donors. It seeks to persuade potential donors that we don't need financial help from them. The fact is we do need their help in the most pressing way.

Have the scare tactics worked?

No. Nor will it. The small donor base in Ireland has largely seen through this tactic, which is just as well for us, otherwise we would not be here today. It's important that the rest of Europe sees through this tactic as well.

Even here I'm appealing to people to come to Tuam, or to our office in Dublin, or log on and make a small donation, or call our Brussels office. For as long as the law allows us, we will protect the identity of those who support us. The only way we could change this would be if all political parties were to agree to publish their donor lists in the future. Then we would obviously do the same. In that case I would suggest that from an agreed future date, all donations – no matter how small – need to come with a name and address and be capped at €1,000 per donor. All political parties should reject and make it illegal to use taxpayers' money to fund political campaigns.

Do you see the need for reform of political donations ?
Of course I do. It is hugely necessary. The same goes for the reform in the area of creating political parties. Anybody should be free to do this.

We should remove the very varied restrictions on the ability to set up political parties in the Union, making them the same for all countries and making the process easy to do and easy as far as compliance is concerned. Politics is the most closely protected 'industry' in Europe. They want no new competition. They should apply the Single Market rules to themselves for a good start.

Indeed, reforms are necessary in funding. All donations should be recorded and names and districts of donors made public. There should be a ceiling of €1,000 on all donations.

This should be the case in all elections and referenda. Obviously, our view is in favour of Member States keeping their own sovereignty rights in the final analysis. We should not concede everything to a superior Brussels government. But we should make politics within Europe a common proposition for all its people. And we should keep the bureaucrats away from meddling. The running of politics should be governed by law and that governance should be comprehensive, open and fair.

Are there other events that have ruffled your feathers?

Quite often, but they smooth down quickly enough. I was giving a speech in the Great Southern Hotel during the campaign, 'A Forum on Europe' debate. At the end of the meeting a Fianna Fail councillor, who had travelled all the way from Cork, came up to me and he said, 'You should know that everything you are saying and doing is being reported back.'

He did not say this in a friendly or joking way. It was an attempt to intimidate. He was marking my cards. I thought for a moment and said, 'If that is the case, then ask Brian Cowen to read the Lisbon Treaty.'

Is there a Declan Ganley 'Witch-hunt'?

There is of course. Witch-hunts of one kind or another are part of politics. In the case of Declan Ganley it has been led by the likes of Micheál Martin and Dick Roche. Elements in the media have also played a part, sometimes a vicious and unfair part.

Is this concentration on No-side funding rather one-sided?

I find it interesting that nobody is probing where the Yes side got their funding – I wouldn't be surprised if they received substantial contributions from Brussels, which would clearly be biased funding.

I'd say that it's pretty obvious to any neutral observer that there is an agenda. This is a shame. At the beginning

I expected at least fairness and balance from newspapers. By being unsubtle in their attacks on Libertas, those who are against us in the media actually undermine their own agenda.

The Irish Times, which I mentioned earlier, may be doing itself some long-term damage here because it has allowed its larger competitor, the *Irish Independent,* along with the *Sunday Times and* the *Irish Mail* and others to become the voice of balance on Irish and European issues. The larger circulation *Irish Independent* is pro-Lisbon editorially but, in fairness to them, they do show some balance. I know a lot of people on both sides of the argument who chuckle at *The Irish Times'* position – it has literally become laughable. It's not too late for this to change and perhaps more balance will manifest itself in the coming months. It would be a shame if this paper – which was the paper of record – loses any more credibility on such an important issue. Amongst other issues, its future readers might look with a jaundiced eye at positions it takes on future issues of the day.

Is it not their right to take a position, either editorially or in comment-pieces?

Of course it is the right of any media outlet to take an editorial position, but they should seek balance in their commentary sections and should eschew vicious and unwarranted attacks.

In terms of what we would see as vicious attacks, it is the lies that one finds hurtful. For example, RTE's *Prime Time* programme was heavily distorted against us. There were subsequent attempts to defend the indefensible, but in my view the programme about me was marked by a real prejudice, and was a low point for the *Prime Time* team.

However, though RTE are openly pro-Lisbon they cannot be accused of having anything approaching the fundamentalism of *The Irish Times*.

How does Ireland compare with Europe generally?

Once you get out of the big fish in a small pond mentality that afflicts a minority in the Irish media, and you get into the European media space, there is a vastly fairer and more professional approach to reporting what we are about. It was coloured somewhat at the beginning by what was coming out of Ireland, but that has now changed. We are receiving fair treatment from many media outlets, ranging from the BBC in the UK, from *Focus* magazine in Germany, and many others. Some of the larger European newspapers have started to give in-depth coverage to what we are actually saying.

Who are your main enemies?

They are those who would attempt to mislead and give succour to people who seek a post-democratic society for Europe.

Then there are minor fringe-players like Junior Minister Dick Roche, Jim Higgins MEP and Jean-Marie Le Pen of the French National Front. They resort to the maddest of conspiracy theories and personal attacks on Libertas and on me personally.

Dick Roche, as a Minister of the Irish Government, has done himself and the country a disservice by his ill-mannered conduct. It does not become the office of a Junior Minister or somebody who claims to respect democracy.

But look, in the greater scheme of things such events are inconsequential. If you are not taking flack you are not over the target. When you hear such shrill attacks coming from those who fear an enlightened, democratic takeover of the anti-democratic power bases in Brussels, you know those same bases see you as the greatest threat to their unaccountable power, and they would be right about that.

There have been rumours circulating about American spooks being associated with your organisation? After all, aren't there several retired high-ranking American and British military individuals on the board of directors of your company, Rivada?

This is one of the madder conspiracy theories. It does not stand up to intelligent scrutiny.

The US answer to the question about supporting Libertas has already been given. On 17 November, 2008, Mr John D. Negroponte, US Deputy Secretary of State, spoke to the Philosophical Society, Trinity College, Dublin. At the end of his presentation, someone in the audience asked the following question:

'In the run-up to what may turn out to be a second Lisbon referendum the provenance of a particular political group here called Libertas and led by Declan Ganley has been called into question. It has been alleged repeatedly that this Declan Ganley group received support from the US Government. Has the Government or the Bush admin-istration provided any support, either financial, moral or otherwise to Declan Ganley and the Libertas movement? I think it would be useful if we could clarify that.'

The Secretary of State replied:

"Absolutely not! I say that on very good authority, not only being Deputy Secretary of State but also being a for-mer Director of National Intelligence. Absolutely not."

By any reasonable measure, this was an authoritative rebuttal. It was sufficient to wipe away allegations that had remained unsubstantiated since April 2008. Unfortunately, no-one reported this episode. The question was worth asking, but the response went unpublished.

The Moderator of the Trinity Philosophical Society was Tom Clonan. He is also a journalist and security analyst of the *Irish Times*. Given the status of Mr. Negroponte, I assume that officials from the Irish Department of Foreign Affairs were also present. One week later the *Prime Time* television programme alluded to the US funding smear and three weeks later the European Parliament made inquiries about it in the US. This Trinity College event and the Negroponte statement have been totally – and, I believe, deliberately – ignored.

Is American involvement in Europe important to you?

My involvement with America is important to me. It goes without saying, America is important to Europe. Have we not seen European leaders making their case to Obama? Have we not got a long-standing relationship with the United States? Is it not the same with the UK and other European powers?

I am an Irishman. I came up with an idea about back-up telecommunications systems in the West of Ireland which I took to America and that was after I had built up a number of businesses across Europe. My team and I built the US side of the business into a relative success and I am not apologising for that.

I am very proud of what we do because it saves lives. Some of the retired military and public safety experts that I have on my Board ensure my business can access some of the very best minds in the world on the issues of public safety communications. It's not my habit to hire second-best. These people have *the* most experience and it's from that experience that you become effective in business. It's important to strive for excellence in whatever you do. And the excellence of my business Board is reflective of my striving for such goals.

How do you see the American connection in your work fitting in with what you say about Europe and about Ireland in Europe?

I'm a proud Irishman. I'm a proud European. We have got to make this place work for its citizens and that's what Libertas is all about. If people think democracy is bad for Europe, then I have a very strong difference of opinion with them.

Democracy needs to be at the heart of everything we do in governance. It was Thomas Jefferson who said that the price of freedom is eternal vigilance. To be properly free we need democracy and we need to guard democracy vigilantly.

We must put ambition back on the agenda in Europe. I genuinely think we have been facilitating and tolerating mediocrity from so-called European leaders. These 'Yes' promoters seem to have some complex relationship with the idea of being European. They cannot answer the simple questions posed about every *diktat* that comes from the opponents of democracy in Brussels. Perhaps they have lost the ability to think for themselves or perhaps they aren't really pro-European at all.

There is a theory that Libertas has a hidden agenda. This is that, by seeking a no vote in the Lisbon Treaty referendum, you wanted to ensure that a European army did not materialise since the powers-that-be in America don't want this to happen.

If you actually listened to what we said, and if you read what I have written, you would immediately realise that this, again, is a blatant lie. I actually support the idea of military integration in Europe as long as it is answerable to a democratically accountable civilian leadership and is supported by the citizens.

A big effort was made to undermine us in the campaign but the result demonstrated its lack of effectiveness. I have always believed that if you tell the truth people will recognise it for what it is. I obviously know a lot of people who voted No and I very strongly suspect that at least a couple of people in the Cabinet, as well as senior people in the Opposition, voted No to Lisbon.

When politicians lie, when they exaggerate and spin, they only end up demeaning themselves. Those that attack us from Brussels and their supporters do seem to have this weird fixation with America and a ridiculous conspiracy theory that America is against the European Union. This, in spite of the fact the Americans – in fairness to them – have been a primary driver behind European unification to the tune of hundreds of billions of dollars over the past number of decades.

They even went so far as to guarantee democracy in Europe and European security through World War I, World War II and the Cold War. Does anyone seriously think that the establishment of democracy across Europe – the defeat of Nazism, Fascism and Communism, the reunification of Germany and the unification of Europe – would have happened when it did without American money and the sacrifice of American lives?

Some of these paranoid critics should visit the war graves across Europe to see the young lads from cities and farms, from Boston to LA, whose young lives were sacrificed for democracy and freedom of Europe. You don't have to be a stooge of anyone to have a touch of gratitude. It's at minimum good manners.

Some of these conspiracy theory attacks on me and Libertas began when they started getting nervous that we were handing out copies of the Lisbon Treaty. That in itself speaks volumes. We were the only ones handing it out. I said to people: 'If you read it – even if you only read the first few pages – you'll know what to do.'

What is the situation now, as we move towards election campaigns and a re-run of the Lisbon Treaty Referendum?

The most obvious thing facing us is that the Government has announced that it will seek to starve Libertas of resources. That will require legislation, since we are now a political party and that changes the rules in our favour. The change in the situation facing us can be seen in the attitude of the Commission on Standards in Public Office.

If you get your mandate and the ability to decide on a future direction for Libertas in the EU, what would be your long-term strategy?

Today – and I hope it is temporary – my view is that Europe is a civilisation in decline. We want to reverse that and energise the population again by giving them back their rights and their ownership of the idea. Voters will change the direction of Europe – not the ponderous collection of 'Yes-Men' at the top.

Over the last year in particular, but for much longer than that, they have shown such poor leadership. When faced with a crisis, they fumble. As far back as Kosovo we saw what a poor grip they had on security matters. With a war on their doorsteps they did not know what to do. It has been even worse with the present financial crisis. Member States have reasserted their sovereignty in face of that because, deep down, there is no real trust in crisis-management by Brussels.

The question is about the future. How does Libertas chart a way forward?

This interview is at least part of your answer. We will not accept what the doom-sayers assert that we are inevitably and irrevocably entering something called 'Post-Democracy', when it is elites and technocrats, not citizens and voters, that decide anything that matters. Although this could be where we end up unless we do something about it. Commission President Barroso and the team he leads are trying to dispense with this time-honoured system of democratic government in Europe, not because it is worn out but because they are.

And your answer to this? It is, after all, overwhelming as a bureaucratic force?

Your words contain the answer. We have got to stop being controlled by bureaucrats, particularly bureaucrats that are capable of presenting us with something as obstructive in its web-like tangle of obscurities and contradictions as the Lisbon Treaty.

We face very serious problems. One of them is the demographic suicide taking place in Europe. For example, in Italy – with current trends – in 50-60 years time most Italians won't know what it is like to have a brother or sister or aunt or uncle.

Do we face a population crisis as well then?

The idea of giving – the donor culture in places like in Ireland and other parts of Europe – is impressive. Care about life is a wonderful emblem of future hope. All EU cultures were once generous in giving and sharing. They were concerned to make sacrifices to bring children into the world and to protect them.

Europe, with significant parts of its population falling, is, to me, a failure of unprecedented historic proportions. What we may be facing is much worse than decimation.

The Black Death in Europe, which changed the face of the continent six centuries ago, did immeasurable damage. But in my view the possible future demographic catastrophe may be far more damaging than the Black Death. Its long-term consequences could be far more severe.

We have all got to take a deep breath and ask what are we going to do. Are we going to do anything or watch our civilisation die? I believe that, in many ways, this is a defining question of our time.

Where does it all begin?

Libertas is challenging the mediocrity of EU leadership. We believe Europe's leaders are taking the people, without their democratic consent or support, into a future that will not work. It is like leading civilisation over a cliff. It is like Stone Age man herding mammoths over an ancient precipice to annihilate them in the supposed interests of a Common Good.

This is not something that Libertas will watch, since it undermines what we believe. That is why we are standing for democracy in the Union, campaigning for democracy and accountability. It is why I am setting out in some detail here my views on what is wrong and what our solutions could be for putting it right.

In another obvious attack on you, certain sections of the media have written articles questioning your nationality.

I'm very much the product of my roots. My 97-year-old grandmother Bridget McHugh (nee Kelly) is still alive and well. This remarkable lady is from the village of Dooega, Achill Island, which is where my mother was born and brought up. When my grandmother was 14 years old she travelled – like so many others from Achill – to Scotland to work as a 'tatie-hoker'. My grandmother picked potatoes for a living.

My great-grandfather was a so-called 'ganger man', who was basically someone managing a group of farm labourers, who lived in something called a bothy, on or near the farm property. These bothies were places where all the farm labourers lived and worked in a communal environment, for the duration of the harvest/planting season etc.

My grandmother moved to London for a job as a maid before the outbreak of World War II. At the onset of the Blitz, my grandmother moved back to Achill and married my grandfather, James McHugh, to bring up five children.

On the Ganley side, my grandfather Jim was born in Manchester to Michael Ganley and Mary Lyons, both from the West of Ireland. The story goes that Michael and Mary eloped to America as Mary's father was not keen on the match. Michael and Mary were married in Boston and, at some point, returned to Manchester and Ireland.

It is not clear, but it seems that two of Mary's brothers were either conscripted or volunteered to join the Irish regiments of the British army at the outbreak of the First World War. And both never returned.

Times were very tough and the family were having a very difficult time, so my grandfather Jim moved back to Ireland when, I think, he was nine-years-old and he brought with him his youngest sister Kitty to live with his aunt and uncle in Lisheen, near Glenamaddy. My great aunt Kitty is thankfully still alive and well today, living in Dunmore, County Galway.

My grandfather quickly became a fluent Irish speaker, as Irish was the only language spoken in Lisheen at the time. His aunt or uncle either couldn't or wouldn't speak English.

Many decades later, in summer days working on the bog with my grandfather, he recounted to me stories he heard from his uncle 'Kip' Ganley – stories that went back to the Famine and are too painful for me to recount here. So many needlessly starved to death within my own village.

Jim Ganley was a great traditional fiddle player and all but one of my uncles picked up that musical gene, which meant that visits home to Lisheen were always truly special events with fireside sessions being a regular feature of times spent with the family. There were four reels that my grandfather played like nobody else – 'The Geese on the Bog,' 'The Frost Is All Over,' 'Lord Gordon's,' and 'The Mason's Apron'. He would roll one into the other and keep playing. I miss him.

My father moved to London from Lisheen to get a job working on the buildings. He ended up becoming a tunneller and then setting up his own construction business. My mother left Achill Island when she was 16 and ended up getting a job in the civil service in London for a period of time. My parents married in Achill and I was born on July 23, 1968 in Watford.

And what of your own upbringing?

I was brought up as an Irish Catholic kid with no doubt of my identity and roots – instilled in me by my grandfathers and my then still alive great grandmother in Achill Island, who I remember in her black shawl, and uncles and aunts who played an important part in my formation as a child. The schools I attended in Watford were Roman Catholic and primarily consisted of children from Irish, Italian, Polish and a smattering of other backgrounds. Being Irish was easy there.

We finally moved home to Ireland when I was almost 13 years old. We had one previous attempt at moving home when I was nine, which didn't work out, but resulted in me living in Achill Island for about eight or nine months. Achill's a great place to be for a nine-year-old, whatever the time of year.

On coming back in the early '80s, I started school at Coláiste Sheosaimh in Glenamaddy. I enjoyed my time there immensely. And I enjoyed my time out of school, working on the farm, the bog, and taking on small jobs even more. It was during this time I developed a real interest in things entrepreneurial, as well as a fascination with history.

I finished my Leaving Cert in 1987 and, like most of my contemporaries at that time, took the boat to England where I started my first job on a building site, supplemented by an evening job in a Cricklewood pub. I didn't spend too long in this sector of the economy and managed to get myself a menial job working for an insurance company.

Shortly afterwards, I made my first trip to Russia where I started my entrepreneurial career, which resulted in my building businesses across Europe, Russia and the US, which varied from forestry to television to telecommunications, as well as other fields.

My businesses have been written about amply in other areas, so I won't prattle on here. The fairest overview they were given – though not perfect – was done by CNBC magazine, two or three years ago, which is available online.

Suffice it to say, I've built businesses in more than 12 countries and more than 17 US States and I am honoured to have worked with remarkably talented people throughout that time. While working in the US, I met my wife Delia in February 1993 and we married in November 1993. It was easily the best decision I ever made. That's not to imply it was my decision (*laughs*), it was just my good fortune that she said 'yes'.

What business achievements are you most proud of?

I'm particularly proud of the team I worked with that was awarded the Louisiana Distinguished Service Medal. The medal was received in recognition of my company (RIVADA Networks) for having saved lives in the aftermath of Hurricane Katrina.

Along the way, in my own small way, I have created many jobs and many opportunities that others have participated in. It was actually while looking for opportunities as an entrepreneur that I heard about the European Constitution and – anticipating that it would develop opportunities for pan-European business – I thought I should read it in anticipation of the great new future and opportunities that Europe would provide. Reading that document changed a lot for me because I started reading it as a businessman but finished reading at as the concerned father of four children.

Finally, is there anything you'd like to sum up with?

I will sum up with this: ultimately, in spite of the challenges, perhaps even because of them, I have enormous optimism for the future of the European Union and of all of the nations within it. I also recognise that for the Union to fulfil its destiny it must harness the wholehearted support of almost half a billion people who call Europe home.

The only legitimate way to make those people fully part of this project is to allow the voice of democracy to be a guiding value that charts our path forward. I have said this from the very beginning of our campaign. Indeed, other politicians have borrowed it: the European project at a minimum has been the most successful peace process in the history of the world. Indeed, it has been much more than that in a positive sense. For example, it has helped to bring the Eastern and Western parts of our continent together after the fall of Communism.

It is essential, not only for smaller countries like Ireland, Latvia or Slovakia, but also for the larger makers of European history, France, Britain, Germany, Italy, Greece, Spain, Portugal, Poland, Sweden, the Netherlands and so on, that we all become part of this together. I truly believe that Europe is capable of a new Renaissance, of leading the world once again.

And where do you start?

The first step to achieving this goal is to recognise that we are capable of it and not only that we are capable of it but that we want to do it. That requires ambition. To feed such ambition we need vision, we need leadership, we need inspiration, and most of all we need the support of the people – ordinary voters – because this must be for them.

There are so many challenges we must face. There is the long-term demographic crisis in Europe which I have already mentioned; this is something that needs to be tackled. It is symptomatic of a larger underlying problem of a loss of hope and understanding amongst people. A civilization that does not invest in its future by being able to reproduce itself is a civilization in terminal decline.

I refuse to accept that Europe is in decline. I am determined to play my part in trying to build a greater European future. I want to ensure, not just that Ireland, but that every other Member State will be part of the just, prosperous, democratic heart and future of Europe.

Are you confident of success?

Success is there for the taking. To achieve it we have to recognise our democratic and cultural origins. We need to know where we come from. We need to see what has made our civilization great. We need to understand the values which have inspired countless generations. We need to recognise again the nobility of the European ideal. And we need to recreate the fact that our continent is a family to which we all belong, where love of mankind is held precious and inviolable.

The tide of history is with us. It is up to us to decide whether we want to flow with it. At the same time we must always remember that individual people come first. We must hold precious the dignity of the hundreds of millions of individual men and women of all ages who make up Europe today, and recognise that love and respect for one another will be the most important key to unlocking humanity's potential.

I will run as a candidate in the European elections, leading other Libertas candidates. We will take seats in the European Parliament and we will chart a new and visionary course for Europe's future. It will be a brave and innovative journey for all of the countries and people of this Union. Europe has given the world its greatest cultural gifts. It has so much more to give.

The message for us all should be, 'Good morning Europe, a new dawn awaits us, let us find the courage and optimism to get up and embrace it.'

INDEX

Reform of EU, Libertas proposals: Commission, 24-25; Commission President, 24; Commission's 3000 working-groups, 70; EU law-making on Council of Ministers, 42, 45; EU Court of Justice, 66-67; European Parliament, 45; new EU laws examined first by National Parliaments, 87; involving National Parliaments in Commission's annual legislative programme, 88; raising a veto on European Council, 48; simpler basic Treaty, 81-82; simplifying presentation of EU laws, 71-72; 'sunset clause' for EU laws, 75; MEPs' payment and expenses, 57-58; single site for European Parliament, 59-61; tackling financial crisis, 94-96, 99-101; subsidies for smaller farm producers, 104; East European budget rebate, 113; cross-EU political parties,140; 'Renaissance universities', 118-19

Rights, see Charter of Fundamental Rights

Rivada, Declan Ganley's telecommunications company, 144, 154

Roche, Dick, Minister for Europe, 49, 78, 129, 141, 143

Services, free movement and workers' rights in Laval and related cases, 65; abortion as an economic service, 63; see Irish Abortion Protocol

Sinnott, Kathy, Independent MEP for Munster(Ireland South), 65

SIPO, Standards in Public Office Commission, 79-80

Subsidies, see lobbyists

Sunday Times, 142

Taxes, Lisbon Treaty provision for EU taxes, 110-11; EU plan for harmonised tax base, 112

Turkey, admission, 131

Veto, non-existent for most EU laws, 38-40; Libertas proposal, 47; unanimity requirement for admission to or expulsion from EU, 132

Voting, Council of Ministers rules under Nice, 37-39; under Lisbon, 40-41; Libertas proposal for electing EU Commissioners, 12-14; for law-making by Council of Ministers, 45; blocking minority, 38; infrequency of voting on Council,37; in European Parliament, 45

Workers' rights, Laval case, 65; and European Socialists, 98

Working groups, preparing EU laws, under Commission, 68; under Council, 35; difficulty in getting information on, 69-70